OSAT

OSAT U.S. History/Oklahoma History/Government/ Economics (017)

SECRETS

Study Guide
Your Key to Exam Success

CEOE Exam Review for the Certification Examinations for Oklahoma Educators/ Oklahoma Subject Area Tests

Dear Future Exam Success Story:

Congratulations on your purchase of our study guide. Our goal in writing our study guide was to cover the content on the test, as well as provide insight into typical test taking mistakes and how to overcome them.

Standardized tests are a key component of being successful, which only increases the importance of doing well in the high-pressure high-stakes environment of test day. How well you do on this test will have a significant impact on your future, and we have the research and practical advice to help you execute on test day.

The product you're reading now is designed to exploit weaknesses in the test itself, and help you avoid the most common errors test takers frequently make.

How to use this study guide

We don't want to waste your time. Our study guide is fast-paced and fluff-free. We suggest going through it a number of times, as repetition is an important part of learning new information and concepts.

First, read through the study guide completely to get a feel for the content and organization. Read the general success strategies first, and then proceed to the content sections. Each tip has been carefully selected for its effectiveness.

Second, read through the study guide again, and take notes in the margins and highlight those sections where you may have a particular weakness.

Finally, bring the manual with you on test day and study it before the exam begins.

Your success is our success

We would be delighted to hear about your success. Send us an email and tell us your story. Thanks for your business and we wish you continued success.

Sincerely,

Mometrix Test Preparation Team

Need more help? Check out our flashcards at: http://MometrixFlashcards.com/CEOE

TABLE OF CONTENTS

Top 20 Test Taking Tips 1
U.S. and Oklahoma History 2
    U.S. History 2
    Oklahoma History 45
Government and Political Science 53
Economics 65
Practice Test 77
    Practice Questions 77
    Answers and Explanations 107
Secret Key #1 - Time is Your Greatest Enemy 124
    Pace Yourself 124
Secret Key #2 - Guessing is not Guesswork 125
    Monkeys Take the Test 125
    $5 Challenge 126
Secret Key #3 - Practice Smarter, Not Harder 127
    Success Strategy 127
Secret Key #4 - Prepare, Don't Procrastinate 128
Secret Key #5 - Test Yourself 129
General Strategies 130
Special Report: How to Overcome Test Anxiety 135
    Lack of Preparation 135
    Physical Signals 136
    Nervousness 136
    Study Steps 138
    Helpful Techniques 139
Additional Bonus Material 144

Top 20 Test Taking Tips

1. Carefully follow all the test registration procedures
2. Know the test directions, duration, topics, question types, how many questions
3. Setup a flexible study schedule at least 3-4 weeks before test day
4. Study during the time of day you are most alert, relaxed, and stress free
5. Maximize your learning style; visual learner use visual study aids, auditory learner use auditory study aids
6. Focus on your weakest knowledge base
7. Find a study partner to review with and help clarify questions
8. Practice, practice, practice
9. Get a good night's sleep; don't try to cram the night before the test
10. Eat a well balanced meal
11. Know the exact physical location of the testing site; drive the route to the site prior to test day
12. Bring a set of ear plugs; the testing center could be noisy
13. Wear comfortable, loose fitting, layered clothing to the testing center; prepare for it to be either cold or hot during the test
14. Bring at least 2 current forms of ID to the testing center
15. Arrive to the test early; be prepared to wait and be patient
16. Eliminate the obviously wrong answer choices, then guess the first remaining choice
17. Pace yourself; don't rush, but keep working and move on if you get stuck
18. Maintain a positive attitude even if the test is going poorly
19. Keep your first answer unless you are positive it is wrong
20. Check your work, don't make a careless mistake

U.S. and Oklahoma History

U.S. History

Well-known Native Americans

The following are five well-known Native Americans and their roles in early US history:
- Squanto, an Algonquian, helped early English settlers survive the hard winter by teaching them the native methods of planting corn, squash, and pumpkins.
- Pocahontas, also Algonquian, became famous as a liaison with John Smith's Jamestown colony in 1607.
- Sacagawea, a Shoshone, served a vital role in the Lewis and Clark expedition when the two explorers hired her as their guide in 1805.
- Crazy Horse and Sitting Bull led Sioux and Cheyenne troops in the Battle of the Little Bighorn in 1876, soundly defeating George Armstrong Custer.
- Chief Joseph, a leader of the Nez Perce who supported peaceful interaction with white settlers, attempted to relocate his tribe to Canada rather than move them to a reservation.

Native American groups

The major regional Native American groups and the major traits of each are as follows:
- The Algonquians in the eastern part of the United States lived in wigwams. The northern tribes subsisted on hunting and gathering, while those who were farther south grew crops such as corn.
- The Iroquois, also an east coast tribe, spoke a different language from the Algonquians, and lived in rectangular longhouses.
- The Plains tribes lived between the Mississippi River and the Rocky Mountains. These nomadic tribes lived in teepees and followed the buffalo herds. Plains tribes included the Sioux, Cheyenne, Comanche and Blackfoot.
- Pueblo tribes included the Zuni, Hopi, and Acoma. They lived in the Southwest deserts in homes made of stone or adobe. They domesticated animals and cultivated corn and beans.
- On the Pacific coast, tribes such as the Tlingit, Chinook and Salish lived on fish as well as deer, native berries and roots. Their rectangular homes housed large family groups, and they used totem poles.
- In the far north, the Aleuts and Inuit lived in skin tents or igloos. Talented fishermen, they built kayaks and umiaks and also hunted caribou, seals, whales and walrus.

Age of Exploration

The Age of Exploration is also called the Age of Discovery. It is generally considered to have begun in the early fifteenth century and continued into the seventeenth century. Major developments of the Age of Exploration included technological advances in navigation, mapmaking and shipbuilding. These advances led to expanded European exploration of the rest of the world. Explorers set out from several European countries, including Portugal, Spain, France and England, seeking new routes to Asia. These efforts led to the discovery of new lands, as well as colonization in India, Asia, Africa, and North America.

> ➤ **Review Video:** Age of Exploration
> *Visit **mometrix.com/academy** and enter **Code**: 167264*

Advancements in navigation and seafaring tools

For long ocean journeys, it was important for sailors to be able to find their way home even when their vessels sailed far out to sea. A variety of navigational tools enabled them to launch ambitious journeys over long distances. The compass and astrolabe were particularly important advancements. The magnetic compass was used by Chinese navigators from approximately 200 B.C.E., and knowledge of the astrolabe came to Europe from Arab navigators and traders who had refined designs developed by the ancient Greeks. The Portuguese developed a ship called a caravel in the 1400s that incorporated navigational advancements with the ability to make long sea journeys. Equipped with this advanced vessel, the Portuguese achieved a major goal of the Age of Exploration by discovering a sea route from Europe to Asia in 1498.

Voyage of Christopher Columbus

In 1492, Columbus, a Genoan explorer, obtained financial backing from King Ferdinand and Queen Isabella of Spain to seek a sea route to Asia. He sought a trade route with the Asian Indies to the west. With three ships, the *Niña*, the *Pinta* and the *Santa Maria*, he eventually landed in the West Indies. While Columbus failed in his effort to discover a western route to Asia, he is credited with the discovery of the Americas.

> ➤ **Review Video: Christopher Columbus**
> *Visit **mometrix.com/academy** and enter Code: 765231*

Colonization of the Americas

France, Spain, the Netherlands, and England each had specific goals in the colonization of the Americas:
- Initial French colonies were focused on expanding the fur trade. Later, French colonization led to the growth of plantations in Louisiana which brought numerous African slaves to the New World.
- Spanish colonists came to look for wealth, and to convert the natives to Christianity. For some, the desire for gold led to mining in the New World, while others established large ranches.

- The Dutch were also involved in the fur trade, and imported slaves as the need for laborers increased.
- British colonists arrived with various goals. Some were simply looking for additional income, while others were fleeing Britain to escape religious persecution.

New England colonies
The New England colonies were New Hampshire, Connecticut, Rhode Island and Massachusetts. These colonies were founded largely to escape religious persecution in England. The beliefs of the Puritans, who migrated to America in the 1600s, significantly influenced the development of these colonies. Situated in the northeast coastal areas of America, the New England colonies featured numerous harbors as well as dense forests. The soil, however, was rocky and had a very short growing season, so was not well suited for agriculture. The economy of New England during the colonial period centered around fishing, shipbuilding and trade along with some small farms and lumber mills. Although some groups congregated in small farms, life centered mainly in towns and cities where merchants largely controlled the trade economy. Coastal cities such as Boston grew and thrived.

Middle or Middle Atlantic Colonies
The Middle or Middle Atlantic Colonies were New York, New Jersey, Pennsylvania and Delaware. Unlike the New England colonies, where most colonists were from England and Scotland, the Middle Colonies founders were from various countries including the Netherlands and Sweden. Various factors led these colonists to America. More fertile than New England, the Middle Colonies became major producers of crops including rye, oats, potatoes, wheat, and barley. Some particularly wealthy inhabitants owned large farms and/or businesses. Farmers in general were able to produce enough to have a surplus to sell. Tenant farmers also rented land from larger land owners.

Southern Colonies
The Southern Colonies were Maryland, Virginia, North Carolina, South Carolina and Georgia. Of the Southern Colonies, Virginia was the first permanent English colony and Georgia the last. The warm climate and rich soil of the south encouraged agriculture, and the growing season was long. As a result, economy in the south was based largely on labor-intensive plantations. Crops included tobacco, rice and indigo, all of which became valuable cash crops. Most land in the south was controlled by wealthy plantation owners and farmers. Labor on the farms came in the form of indentured servants and African slaves. The first of these African slaves arrived in Virginia in 1619.

French and Indian Wars

The British defeat of the Spanish Armada in 1588 led to the decline of Spanish power in Europe. This in turn led the British and French into battle several times between 1689 and 1748. These wars were:
- King William's War, or the Nine Years War, 1689-1697. This war was fought largely in Flanders.
- The War of Spanish Succession, or Queen Anne's War, 1702-1713
- War of Austrian Succession, or King George's War, 1740-1748

The fourth and final war, the French and Indian War (1754-1763), was fought largely in the North American territory, and resulted in the end of France's reign as a colonial power in

North America. Although the French held many advantages, including more cooperative colonists and numerous Indian allies, the strong leadership of William Pitt eventually led the British to victory. Costs incurred during the wars eventually led to discontent in the colonies and helped spark the American Revolution.

Navigation Acts

The Navigation Acts, enacted in 1651, were an attempt by Britain to dominate international trade. Aimed largely at the Dutch, the Acts banned foreign ships from transporting goods to the British colonies, and from transporting goods to Britain from elsewhere in Europe. While the restrictions on trade angered some colonists, these Acts were helpful to other American colonists who, as members of the British Empire, were legally able to provide ships for Britain's growing trade interests and use the ships for their own trading ventures. By the time the French and Indian War had ended, one-third of British merchant ships were built in the American colonies. Many colonists amassed fortunes in the shipbuilding trade.

Higher taxes after the French and Indian War

The French and Indian War created circumstances for which the British desperately needed more revenue. These needs included:
- Paying off the war debt
- Defending the expanding empire
- Governing Britain's 33 far-flung colonies, including the American colonies

To meet these needs, the British passed additional laws, increasing revenues from the colonies. Because they had spent so much money to defend the American colonies, the British felt it was appropriate to collect considerably higher taxes from them. The colonists felt this was unfair, and many were led to protest the increasing taxes. Eventually, protest led to violence.

Triangular trade

Triangular trade began in the Colonies with ships setting off for Africa, carrying rum. In Africa, the rum was traded for gold or slaves. Ships then went from Africa to the West Indies, trading slaves for sugar, molasses, or money. To complete the triangle, the ships returned to the colonies with sugar or molasses to make more rum, as well as stores of gold and silver. This trade triangle violated the Molasses Act of 1733, which required the colonists to pay high duties to Britain on molasses acquired from French, Dutch, and Spanish colonies. The colonists ignored these duties, and the British government adopted a policy of salutary neglect by not enforcing them.

Effects of new laws on British-Colonial relations

While earlier revenue-generating acts such as the Navigation Acts brought money to the colonists, the new laws after 1763 required colonists to pay money back to Britain. The British felt this was fair since the colonists were British subjects and since they had incurred debt protecting the Colonies. The colonists felt it was not only unfair, but illegal.

The development of local government in America had given the colonists a different view of the structure and role of government. This made it difficult for the British to understand the

- 5 -

colonists' protests against what the British felt was a fair and reasonable solution to the mother country's financial problems.

Increasing discontent in the American colonies

More and more colonists were born on American soil, decreasing any sense of kinship with the far away British rulers. Their new environment had led to new ideas of government and a strong view of the colonies as a separate entity from Britain. Colonists were allowed to self-govern in domestic issues, but Britain controlled international issues. In fact, the American colonies were largely left to form their own local government bodies, giving them more freedom than any other colonial territory. This gave the colonists a sense of independence, which led them to resent control from Britain. Threats during the French and Indian War led the colonists to call for unification in order to protect themselves.

Difference between colonial government and British government

As new towns and other legislative districts developed in America, the colonists began to practice representative government. Colonial legislative bodies were made up of elected representatives chosen by male property owners in the districts. These individuals represented the interests of the districts from which they had been elected. By contrast, in Britain the Parliament represented the entire country. Parliament was not elected to represent individual districts. Instead, they represented specific classes. Because of this drastically different approach to government, the British did not understand the colonists' statement that they had no representation in the British Parliament.

Acts of British Parliament

After the French and Indian Wars, the British Parliament passed four major acts:
- The Sugar Act, 1764—this act not only required taxes to be collected on molasses brought into the colonies, but gave British officials the right to search the homes of anyone suspected of violating it.
- The Stamp Act, 1765—this act taxed printed materials such as newspapers and legal documents. Protests led the Stamp Act to be repealed in 1766, but the repeal also included the Declaratory Act, which stated that Parliament had the right to govern the colonies.
- The Quartering Act, 1765—this act required colonists to provide accommodations and supplies for British troops. In addition, colonists were prohibited from settling west of the Appalachians until given permission by Britain.
- The Townshend Acts, 1767—these acts taxed paper, paint, lead and tea that came into the colonies. Colonists led boycotts in protest, and in Massachusetts leaders like Samuel and John Adams began to organize resistance against British rule.

Boston Massacre

With the passage of the Stamp Act, nine colonies met in New York to demand its repeal. Elsewhere, protest arose in New York City, Philadelphia, Boston and other cities. These protests sometimes escalated into violence, often targeting ruling British officials. The passage of the Townshend Acts in 1767 led to additional tension in the colonies. The British sent troops to New York City and Boston. On March 5, 1770, protesters began to taunt the British troops, throwing snowballs. The soldiers responded by firing into the crowd. This clash between protesters and soldiers led to five deaths and eight injuries, and was christened the Boston Massacre. Shortly thereafter, Britain repealed the majority of the Townshend Acts.

Tea Act and the Boston Tea Party

The majority of the Townshend Acts were repealed after the Boston Massacre in 1770, but Britain kept the tax on tea. In 1773, the Tea Act was passed. This allowed the East India Company to sell tea for much lower prices, and also allowed them to bypass American distributors, selling directly to shopkeepers instead. Colonial tea merchants saw this as a direct assault on their business. In December of 1773, the Sons of Liberty boarded ships in Boston Harbor and dumped 342 chests of tea into the sea in protest of the new laws. This act of protest came to be known as the Boston Tea Party.

Coercive/Intolerable Acts

The Coercive Acts passed by Britain in 1774 were meant to punish Massachusetts for defying British authority. The four acts, also known as the Intolerable Acts:
- Shut down ports in Boston until the city paid back the value of the tea destroyed during the Boston Tea Party
- Required that local government officials in Massachusetts be appointed by the governor rather than being elected by the people
- Allowed trials of British soldiers to be transferred to Britain rather than being held in Massachusetts
- Required locals to provide lodging for British soldiers any time there was a disturbance, even if lodging required them to stay in private homes

These Acts led to the assembly of the First Continental Congress in Philadelphia on September 5, 1774. Fifty-five delegates met, representing 12 of the American colonies. They sought compromise with England over England's increasingly harsh efforts to control the colonies.

First Continental Congress

The First Continental Congress met in Philadelphia on September 5, 1774. Their goal was to achieve a peaceful agreement with Britain. Made up of delegates from 12 of the 13 colonies, the Congress affirmed loyalty to Britain and the power of Parliament to dictate foreign affairs in the colonies. However, they demanded that the Intolerable Acts be repealed, and instituted a trade embargo with Britain until this came to pass.

In response, George III of England declared that the American colonies must submit or face military action. The British sought to end assemblies that opposed their policies. These assemblies gathered weapons and began to form militias. On April 19, 1775, the British military was ordered to disperse a meeting of the Massachusetts Assembly. A battle ensued on Lexington Common as the armed colonists resisted. The resulting battles became the Battle of Lexington and Concord—the first battles of the American Revolution.

Second Continental Congress

The Second Continental Congress met in Philadelphia on May 10, 1775, a month after Lexington and Concord. Their discussions centered on defense of the American colonies and how to conduct the growing war, as well as local government. The delegates also discussed declaring independence from Britain, with many members in favor of this drastic move. They established an army, and on June 15, named George Washington as its commander-in-chief. By 1776, it was obvious that there was no turning back from full-scale war with Britain. The colonial delegates of the Continental Congress drafted the Declaration of Independence on July 4, 1776.

Declaration of Independence

Penned by Thomas Jefferson and signed on July 4, 1776, the Declaration of Independence stated that King George III had violated the rights of the colonists and was establishing a tyrannical reign over them. Many of Jefferson's ideas of natural rights and property rights were shaped by seventeenth-century philosopher John Locke. Jefferson asserted all people's rights to "life, liberty and the pursuit of happiness." Locke's comparable idea asserted "life, liberty, and private property." Both felt that the purpose of government was to protect the rights of the people, and that individual rights were more important than individuals' obligations to the state.

Battles of the Revolutionary War

The following are five major battles of the Revolutionary War and their significance:
- The Battle of Lexington and Concord (April 1775) is considered the first engagement of the Revolutionary War.
- The Battle of Bunker Hill (June 1775) was one of the bloodiest of the entire war. Although American troops withdrew, about half of the British army was lost. The colonists proved they could stand against professional British soldiers. In August, Britain declared that the American colonies were officially in a state of rebellion.
- The first colonial victory occurred in Trenton, New Jersey, when Washington and his troops crossed the Delaware River on Christmas Day, 1776 for a December 26 surprise attack on British and Hessian troops.
- The Battle of Saratoga effectively ended a plan to separate the New England colonies from their Southern counterparts. The surrender of British general John Burgoyne led to France joining the war as allies of the Americans, and is generally considered a turning point of the war.
- On October 19, 1781, General Cornwallis surrendered after a defeat in the Battle of Yorktown, ending the Revolutionary War.

Treaty of Paris

The Treaty of Paris was signed on September 3, 1783, bringing an official end to the Revolutionary War. In this document, Britain officially recognized the United States of America as an independent nation. The treaty established the Mississippi River as the country's western border. The treaty also restored Florida to Spain, while France reclaimed African and Caribbean colonies seized by the British in 1763. On November 25, 1783, the last British troops departed from the newly born United States of America.

Articles of Confederation

A precursor to the Constitution, the Articles of Confederation represented the first attempt of the newly independent colonies to establish the basics of government. The Continental

Congress approved the Articles on November 15, 1777. They went into effect on March 1, 1781, following ratification by the thirteen states. The Articles prevented a central government from gaining too much power, instead giving power to a Congressional body made up of delegates from all thirteen states. However, the individual states retained final authority.

Without a strong central executive, though, this weak alliance among the new states proved ineffective in settling disputes or enforcing laws. The idea of a weak central government needed to be revised. Recognition of these weaknesses eventually led to the drafting of a new document, the Constitution.

The Constitution

Delegates from twelve of the thirteen states (Rhode Island was not represented) met in Philadelphia in May of 1787, initially intending to revise the Articles of Confederation. However, it quickly became apparent that a simple revision would not provide the workable governmental structure the newly formed country needed. After vowing to keep all the proceedings secret until the final document was completed, the delegates set out to draft what would eventually become the Constitution of the United States of America. By keeping the negotiations secret, the delegates were able to present a completed document to the country for ratification, rather than having every small detail hammered out by the general public.

Structure of proposed government

The delegates agreed that the new nation required a strong central government, but that its overall power should be limited. The various branches of the government should have balanced power, so that no one group could control the others. Final power belonged with the citizens who voted officials into office based on who would provide the best representation.

Virginia Plan, New Jersey Plan, and the Great Compromise

Disagreement immediately occurred between delegates from large states and those from smaller states. James Madison and Edmund Randolph (the governor of Virginia) felt that representation in Congress should be based on state population. This was the Virginia Plan. The New Jersey Plan, presented by William Paterson, from New Jersey, proposed each state have equal representation. Finally, Roger Sherman from Connecticut formulated the Connecticut Compromise, also called the Great Compromise. The result was the familiar structure we have today. Each state has the equal representation of two Senators in the Senate, with the number of representatives in the House of Representatives based on population. This is called a bicameral Congress. Both houses may draft bills, but financial matters must originate in the House of Representatives.

Three-fifths compromise

During debate on the US Constitution, a disagreement arose between the Northern and Southern states involving how slaves should be counted when determining a state's quota of representatives. In the South large numbers of slaves were commonly used to run plantations. Delegates wanted slaves to be counted to determine the number of representatives, but not counted to determine the amount of taxes the states would pay. The Northern states wanted exactly the opposite arrangement. The final decision was to count three-fifths of the slave population both for tax purposes and to determine representation. This was called the three-fifths compromise.

Commerce Compromise

The Commerce Compromise also resulted from a North/South disagreement. In the North the economy was centered on industry and trade. The Southern economy was largely agricultural. The Northern states wanted to give the new government the ability to regulate exports as well as trade between the states. The South opposed this plan. Another compromise was in order. In the end, Congress received regulatory power over all trade, including the ability to collect tariffs on exported goods. In the South, this raised another red flag regarding the slave trade, as they were concerned about the effect on their economy if tariffs were levied on slaves. The final agreement allowed importing slaves to continue for twenty years without government intervention. Import taxes on slaves were limited, and after the year 1808, Congress could decide whether to allow continued imports of slaves.

Objections against the Constitution

Once the Constitution was drafted, it was presented for approval by the states. Nine states needed to approve the document for it to become official. However, debate and discussion continued. Major concerns included:
- The lack of a bill of rights to protect individual freedoms
- States felt too much power was being handed over to the central government
- Voters wanted more control over their elected representatives

Discussion about necessary changes to the Constitution was divided into two camps: Federalists and Anti-Federalists. Federalists wanted a strong central government. Anti-Federalists wanted to prevent a tyrannical government from developing if a central government held too much power.

Federalist and Anti-Federalist camps

Major Federalist leaders included Alexander Hamilton, John Jay and James Madison. They wrote a series of letters, called the Federalist Papers, aimed at convincing the states to ratify the Constitution. These were published in New York papers. Anti-Federalists included Thomas Jefferson and Patrick Henry. They argued against the Constitution as it was originally drafted in a series of Anti-Federalist Papers.

The final compromise produced a strong central government controlled by checks and balances. A Bill of Rights was also added, becoming the first ten amendments to the Constitution. These amendments protected rights such as freedom of speech, freedom of religion, and other basic rights. Aside from various amendments added throughout the years, the United States Constitution has remained unchanged.

Administration of the new government

The individuals who formed the first administration of the new government were:
- George Washington—elected as the first President of the United States in 1789
- John Adams—finished second in the election and became the first Vice President
- Thomas Jefferson—appointed by Washington as Secretary of State
- Alexander Hamilton—appointed Secretary of the Treasury

Alien and Sedition Acts

When John Adams became president, a war was raging between Britain and France. While Adams and the Federalists backed the British, Thomas Jefferson and the Republican Party supported the French. The United States nearly went to war with France during this time period, while France worked to spread its international standing and influence under the leadership of Napoleon Bonaparte. The Alien and Sedition Acts grew out of this conflict, and made it illegal to speak in a hostile fashion against the existing government. They also allowed the president to deport anyone in the US who was not a citizen and who was suspected of treason or treasonous activity. When Jefferson became the third president in 1800, he repealed these four laws and pardoned anyone who had been convicted under them.

> ➤ **Review Video:** The Alien and Sedition Acts
> *Visit **mometrix.com/academy** and enter **Code: 633780***

Political parties

Many in the US were against political parties after seeing the way parties, or factions, functioned in Britain. The factions in Britain were more interested in personal profit than the overall good of the country, and they did not want this to happen in the US.

However, the differences of opinion between Thomas Jefferson and Alexander Hamilton led to formation of political parties. Hamilton favored a stronger central government, while Jefferson felt that more power should remain with the states. Jefferson was in favor of strict Constitutional interpretation, while Hamilton believed in a more flexible approach. As others joined the two camps, Hamilton backers began to term themselves Federalists while those supporting Jefferson became identified as Democratic-Republicans.

Whig Party, Democratic Party, and Republican Party

Thomas Jefferson was elected president in 1800 and again in 1804. The Federalist Party began to decline, and its major figure, Alexander Hamilton, died in a duel with Aaron Burr in 1804. By 1816, the Federalist Party had virtually disappeared.

New parties sprang up to take its place. After 1824, the Democratic-Republican Party suffered a split. The Whigs rose, backing John Quincy Adams and industrial growth. The new Democratic Party formed, in opposition to the Whigs, and their candidate, Andrew Jackson, was elected as president in 1828.

By the 1850s, issues regarding slavery led to the formation of the Republican Party, which was anti-slavery, while the Democratic Party, with a larger interest in the South, favored slavery. This Republican/Democrat division formed the basis of today's two-party system.

Marbury v. Madison

The main duty of the Supreme Court today is judicial review. This power was largely established by Marbury v. Madison. When John Adams was voted out of office in 1800, he worked, during his final days in office, to appoint Federalist judges to Supreme Court positions, knowing Jefferson, his replacement, held opposing views. As late as March 3, the day before Jefferson was to take office, Adams made last-minute appointments referred to as "Midnight Judges." One of the late appointments was William Marbury. The next day, March 4, Jefferson ordered his Secretary of State, James Madison, not to deliver Marbury's commission. This decision was backed by Chief Justice Marshall, who determined that the Judiciary Act of 1789, which granted the power to deliver commissions, was illegal in that it gave the Judicial Branch powers not granted in the Constitution. This case set precedent for the Supreme Court to nullify laws it found to be unconstitutional.

> ➤ **Review Video:** Marbury v. Madison
> *Visit **mometrix.com/academy** and enter **Code: 270990***

McCulloch v. Maryland

Judicial review was further exercised by the Supreme Court in McCulloch v. Maryland. When Congress chartered a national bank, the Second Bank of the United States, Maryland voted to tax any bank business dealing with banks chartered outside the state, including the federally chartered bank. Andrew McCulloch, an employee of the Second Bank of the US in Baltimore, refused to pay this tax. The resulting lawsuit from the State of Maryland went to the Supreme Court for judgment.

John Marshall, Chief Justice of the Supreme Court, stated that Congress was within its rights to charter a national bank. In addition, the State of Maryland did not have the power to levy a tax on the federal bank or on the federal government in general. In cases where state and federal government collided, precedent was set for the federal government to prevail.

Effects of the Treaty of Paris on Native Americans

After the Revolutionary War, the Treaty of Paris, which outlined the terms of surrender of the British to the Americans, granted large parcels of land to the US that were occupied by Native Americans. The new government attempted to claim the land, treating the natives as a conquered people. This approach proved unenforceable.

Next, the government tried purchasing the land from the Indians via a series of treaties as the country expanded westward. In practice, however, these treaties were not honored, and Native Americans were simply dislocated and forced to move farther and farther west, often with military action, as American expansion continued.

Indian Removal Act of 1830 and the Treaty of New Echota

The Indian Removal Act of 1830 gave the new American government power to form treaties with Native Americans. In theory, America would claim land east of the Mississippi in exchange for land west of the Mississippi, to which the natives would relocate voluntarily. In practice, many tribal leaders were forced into signing the treaties, and relocation at times occurred by force. The Treaty of New Echota in 1835 was supposedly a treaty between the US government and Cherokee tribes in Georgia. However, the treaty was not signed by tribal leaders, but rather by a small portion of the represented people. The leaders protested and refused to leave, but President Martin Van Buren enforced the treaty by sending soldiers. During their forced relocation, more than 4,000 Cherokee Indians died on what became known as the Trail of Tears.

Early economic trends by region

In the Northeast, the economy mostly depended on manufacturing, industry, and industrial development. This led to a dichotomy between rich business owners and industrial leaders and the much poorer workers who supported their businesses. The South continued to depend on agriculture, especially on large-scale farms or plantations worked mostly by slaves and indentured servants. In the West, where new settlements had begun to develop, the land was largely wild. Growing communities were essentially agricultural, raising crops and livestock. The differences between regions led each to support different interests both politically and economically.

Louisiana Purchase

With tension still high between France and Britain, Napoleon was in need of money to support his continuing war efforts. To secure necessary funds, he decided to sell the Louisiana Territory to the US President Thomas Jefferson wanted to buy New Orleans, feeling US trade was made vulnerable to both Spain and France at that port. Instead, Napoleon sold him the entire territory for the bargain price of fifteen million dollars. The Louisiana Territory was larger than all the rest of the United States put together, and it eventually became fifteen additional states. Federalists in Congress were opposed to the purchase. They feared that the Louisiana Purchase would extend slavery, and that further western growth would weaken the power of the northern states.

Early foreign policy

The three major ideas driving American foreign policy during its early years were:
- Isolationism—the early US government did not intend to establish colonies, though they did plan to grow larger within the bounds of North America.
- No entangling alliances—both George Washington and Thomas Jefferson were opposed to forming any permanent alliances with other countries or becoming involved in other countries' internal issues.
- Nationalism—a positive patriotic feeling about the United States blossomed quickly among its citizens, particularly after the War of 1812, when the US once again defeated Britain. The Industrial Revolution also sparked increased nationalism by allowing even the most far-flung areas of the US to communicate with each other via telegraph and the expanding railroad.

War of 1812

The War of 1812 grew out of the continuing tension between France and Great Britain. Napoleon continued striving to conquer Britain, while the US continued trade with both countries, but favored France and the French colonies. Because of what Britain saw as an alliance between America and France, they determined to bring an end to trade between the two nations.

With the British preventing US trade with the French and the French preventing trade with the British, James Madison's presidency introduced acts to regulate international trade. If either Britain or France removed their restrictions, America would not trade with the other country. Napoleon acted first, and Madison prohibited trade with England. England saw this as the US formally siding with the French, and war ensued in 1812.

The War of 1812 has been called the Second American Revolution. It established the superiority of the US naval forces and reestablished US independence from Britain and Europe.

The British had two major objections to America's continued trade with France. First, they saw the US as helping France's war effort by providing supplies and goods. Second, the United States had grown into a competitor, taking trade and money away from British ships and tradesmen. In its attempts to end American trade with France, the British put into effect the Orders in Council, which made any and all French-owned ports off-limits to American ships. They also began to seize American ships and conscript their crews.

> ➤ **Review Video:** Opinions About the War of 1812
> *Visit **mometrix.com/academy** and enter **Code**: **274558***

> ➤ **Review Video:** Results of the War of 1812
> *Visit **mometrix.com/academy** and enter **Code**: **993725***

Military events

Two major naval battles, at Lake Erie and Lake Champlain, kept the British from invading the US via Canada. American attempts to conquer Canadian lands were not successful.

In another memorable British attack, the British invaded Washington DC and burned the White House on August 24, 1814. Legend has it that Dolley Madison, the First Lady, salvaged the portrait of George Washington from the fire. On Christmas Eve, 1814, the Treaty of Ghent officially ended the war. However, Andrew Jackson, unaware that the war was over, managed another victory at New Orleans on January 8, 1815. This victory improved American morale and led to a new wave of national pride and support known as the "Era of Good Feelings."

Monroe Doctrine

On December 2, 1823, President Monroe delivered a message to Congress in which he introduced the Monroe Doctrine. In this address, he stated that any attempts by European powers to establish new colonies on the North American continent would be considered interference in American politics. The US would stay out of European matters, and expected

Europe to offer America the same courtesy. This approach to foreign policy stated in no uncertain terms that America would not tolerate any new European colonies in the New World, and that events occurring in Europe would no longer influence the policies and doctrines of the US.

Lewis and Clark Expedition

The purchase of the Louisiana Territory from France in 1803 more than doubled the size of the United States. President Thomas Jefferson wanted to have the area mapped and explored, since much of the territory was wilderness. He chose Meriwether Lewis and William Clark to head an expedition into the Louisiana Territory. After two years, Lewis and Clark returned, having traveled all the way to the Pacific Ocean. They brought maps, detailed journals, and a multitude of information about the wide expanse of land they had traversed. The Lewis and Clark Expedition opened up the west in the Louisiana Territory and beyond for further exploration and settlement.

> ➤ **Review Video:** The Lewis and Clark Expedition
> Visit ***mometrix.com/academy*** and enter ***Code*: 241256**

Manifest Destiny

In the 1800s, many believed America was destined by God to expand west, bringing as much of the North American continent as possible under the umbrella of US government. With the Northwest Ordinance and the Louisiana Purchase, over half of the continent became American. However, the rapid and relentless expansion brought conflict with the Native Americans, Great Britain, Mexico and Spain. One result of "Manifest Destiny" was the Mexican-American War from 1846 to 1848. By the end of the war, Texas, California, and a large portion of what is now the American Southwest joined the growing nation. Conflict also arose over the Oregon territory, shared by the US and Britain. In 1846, President James Polk resolved this problem by compromising with Britain, establishing a US boundary south of the 49th parallel.

> ➤ **Review Video:** Manifest Destiny
> Visit ***mometrix.com/academy*** and enter ***Code*: 962946**

Mexican-American War

Spain had held colonial interests in America since the 1540s—earlier even than Great Britain. In 1810, Mexico revolted against Spain and became a free nation in 1821. Texas followed suit, declaring its independence after an 1836 revolution. In 1844, the Democrats pressed President Tyler to annex Texas. Unlike his predecessor, Andrew Jackson, Tyler agreed to admit Texas into the Union and in 1845 Texas became a state.

During Mexico's war for independence, the nation incurred $4.5 million in war debts to the US Polk offered to forgive the debts in return for New Mexico and Upper California, but Mexico refused. In 1846, war was declared in response to a Mexican attack on American troops along the southern border of Texas. Additional conflict arose in Congress over the Wilmot Proviso, which proposed banning of slavery from any territory the US acquired from Mexico. The war ended in 1848.

Gadsden Purchase and the 1853 post-war treaty with Mexico

After the Mexican-American war, a second treaty in 1853 determined hundreds of miles of America's southwest borders. In 1854, the Gadsden Purchase was finalized, providing even more territory to aid in the building of the transcontinental railroad. This purchase added what would eventually become the southernmost regions of Arizona and New Mexico to the growing nation. The modern outline of the United States was by this time nearly complete.

American System

Spurred by the trade conflicts of the War of 1812, and supported by Henry Clay among others, the American System set up tariffs to help protect American interests from competition with overseas products. Reducing competition led to growth in employment and an overall increase in American industry. The higher tariffs also provided funds for the government to pay for various improvements. Congress passed high tariffs in 1816 and also chartered a federal bank. The Second Bank of the United States was given the job of regulating America's money supply.

Jacksonian Democracy

Jacksonian Democracy is largely seen as a shift from politics favoring the wealthy to politics favoring the common man. All free white males were given the right to vote, not just property owners, as had been the case previously. Jackson's approach favored the patronage system, Laissez-faire economics, and relocation of the Indian tribes from the Southeast portion of the country. Jackson opposed the formation of a federal bank and allowed the Second Band of the United States to collapse by vetoing a bill to renew the charter. Jackson also faced the challenge of the Nullification Crisis when South Carolina claimed that it could ignore or nullify any federal law it considered unconstitutional. Jackson sent troops to the state to enforce the protested tariff laws, and a compromise engineered by Henry Clay in 1833 settled the matter for the time being.

> ➤ **Review Video:** Andrew Jackson as President
> *Visit **mometrix.com/academy** and enter **Code: 667792***

> ➤ **Review Video:** Major Issues Under Andrew Jackson
> *Visit **mometrix.com/academy** and enter **Code: 739251***

Conflict between North and South

The conflict between North and South coalesced around the issue of slavery, but other elements contributed to the growing disagreement. Though most farmers in the South worked small farms with little or no slave labor, the huge plantations run by the South's rich depended on slaves or indentured servants to remain profitable. They had also become more dependent on cotton, with slave populations growing in concert with the rapid increase in cotton production. In the North, a more diverse agricultural economy and the growth of industry made slaves rarer. The abolitionist movement grew steadily, with

Harriet Beecher Stowe's *Uncle Tom's Cabin* giving many an idea to rally around. A collection of anti-slavery organizations formed, with many actively working to free slaves in the South, often bringing them to the northern states or Canada.

> ➢ **Review Video:** <u>Conflict between the North and South</u>
> Visit *mometrix.com/academy* and enter *Code*: **219819**

Anti-slavery organizations

Five anti-slavery organizations and their significance are:
- American Colonization Society—Protestant churches formed this group, aimed at returning black slaves to Africa. Former slaves subsequently formed Liberia, but the colony did not do well, as the region was not well-suited for agriculture.
- American Anti-Slavery Society—William Lloyd Garrison, a Quaker, was the major force behind this group and its newspaper, *The Liberator*.
- Philadelphia Female Anti-Slavery Society—a women-only group formed by Margaretta Forten because women were not allowed to join the Anti-Slavery Society formed by her father.
- Anti-Slavery Convention of American Women—this group continued meeting even after pro-slavery factions burned down their original meeting place.
- Female Vigilant Society—an organization that raised funds to help the Underground Railroad, as well as slave refugees.

Attitudes toward education

Horace Mann, among others, felt that schools could help children become better citizens, keep them away from crime, prevent poverty, and help American society become more unified. His *Common School Journal* brought his ideas of the importance of education into the public consciousness and proposed his suggestions for an improved American education system. Increased literacy led to increased awareness of current events, Western expansion, and other major developments of the time period. Public interest and participation in the arts and literature also increased. By the end of the 19th century, all children had access to a free public elementary education.

Transportation

As America expanded its borders, it also developed new technology to travel the rapidly growing country. Roads and railroads traversed the nation, with the Transcontinental Railroad eventually allowing travel from one coast to the other. Canals and steamboats simplified water travel and made shipping easier and less expensive. The Erie Canal (1825) connected the Great Lakes with the Hudson River. Other canals connected other major waterways, further facilitating transportation and the shipment of goods.

With growing numbers of settlers moving into the West, wagon trails developed, including the Oregon Trail, California Trail and the Santa Fe Trail. The most common vehicles seen along these westbound trails were covered wagons, also known as prairie schooners.

Industrial activity and major inventions

During the eighteenth century, goods were often manufactured in houses or small shops. With increased technology allowing for the use of machines, factories began to develop. In factories a large volume of salable goods could be produced in a much shorter amount of time. Many Americans, including increasing numbers of immigrants, found jobs in these factories, which were in constant need of labor. Another major invention was the cotton gin, which significantly decreased the processing time of cotton and was a major factor in the rapid expansion of cotton production in the South.

Labor movements

In 1751, a group of bakers held a protest in which they stopped baking bread. This was technically the first American labor strike. In the 1830s and 1840s, labor movements began in earnest. Boston's masons, carpenters and stoneworkers protested the length of the workday, fighting to reduce it to ten hours. In 1844, a group of women in the textile industry also fought to reduce their workday to ten hours, forming the Lowell Female Labor Reform Association. Many other protests occurred and organizations developed through this time period with the same goal in mind.

Second Great Awakening

Led by Protestant evangelical leaders, the Second Great Awakening occurred between 1800 and 1830. Several missionary groups grew out of the movement, including the American Home Missionary Society, which formed in 1826. The ideas behind the Second Great Awakening focused on personal responsibility, both as an individual and in response to injustice and suffering. The American Bible Society and the American Tract Society provided literature, while various traveling preachers spread the word. New denominations arose, including the Latter-day Saints and Seventh-day Adventists.

Another movement associated with the Second Great Awakening was the temperance movement, focused on ending the production and use of alcohol. One major organization behind the temperance movement was the Society for the Promotion of Temperance, formed in 1826 in Boston.

Women's rights movement

The women's rights movement began in the 1840s with leaders including Elizabeth Cady Stanton, Sojourner Truth, Ernestine Rose, and Lucretia Mott. In 1869, Elizabeth Cady Stanton and Susan B. Anthony formed the National Woman Suffrage Association, fighting for women's right to vote.

In 1848 in Seneca Falls, the first women's rights convention was held, with about three hundred attendees. The two-day Seneca Falls Convention discussed the rights of women to vote (suffrage) as well as equal treatment in careers, legal proceedings, etc. The convention produced a "Declaration of Sentiments" which outlined a plan for women to attain the rights they deserved. Frederick Douglass supported the women's rights movement, as well as the abolition movement. In fact, women's rights and abolition movements often went hand-in-hand during this time period.

Missouri Compromise

By 1819, the United States had developed a tenuous balance between slave and free states, with exactly twenty-two senators in Congress from each faction. However, Missouri was ready to join the union. As a slave state, it would tip the balance in Congress. To prevent this imbalance, the Missouri Compromise brought the northern part of Massachusetts into the union as Maine, establishing it as a free state to balance the admission of Missouri as a slave state. In addition, the remaining portion of the Louisiana Purchase was to remain free north of latitude 36°30'. Since cotton did not grow well this far north, this limitation was acceptable to congressmen representing the slave states.

However, the proposed Missouri constitution presented a problem, as it outlawed immigration of free blacks into the state. Another compromise was in order, this time proposed by Henry Clay. According to this new compromise, Missouri's would never pass a law that prevented anyone from entering the state. Through this and other work, Clay earned his title of the "Great Compromiser."

> **Review Video:** Missouri Compromise
> Visit *mometrix.com/academy* and enter *Code*: **848091**

Popular sovereignty and the Compromise of 1850

In addition to the pro-slavery and anti-slavery factions, a third group rose who felt that each individual state should decide whether to allow or permit slavery within its borders. The idea that a state could make its own choices was referred to as popular sovereignty.

When California applied to join the union in 1849, the balance of congressional power was again threatened. The Compromise of 1850 introduced a group of laws meant to bring an end to the conflict:
- California's admittance as a free state
- The outlaw of the slave trade in Washington, D.C
- An increase in efforts to capture escaped slaves
- The right of New Mexico and Utah territories to decide individually whether to allow slavery

In spite of these measures, debate raged each time a new state prepared to enter the union.

Kansas-Nebraska Act

With the creation of the Kansas and Nebraska territories in 1854, another debate began. Congress allowed popular sovereignty in these territories, but slavery opponents argued that the Missouri Compromise had already made slavery illegal in this region. In Kansas, two separate governments arose, one pro-slavery and one anti-slavery. Conflict between the two factions rose to violence, leading Kansas to gain the nickname of "Bleeding Kansas."

> **Review Video:** Sectional Crisis: The Kansas-Nebraska Act
> Visit *mometrix.com/academy* and enter *Code*: **982119**

Dred Scott decision

Abolitionist factions coalesced around the case of Dred Scott, using his case to test the country's laws regarding slavery. Scott, a slave, had been taken by his owner from Missouri, which was a slave state. He then traveled to Illinois, a free state, then on to the Minnesota Territory, also free based on the Missouri Compromise. After several years, he returned to Missouri and his owner subsequently died. Abolitionists took Scott's case to court, stating that Scott was no longer a slave but free, since he had lived in free territory. The case went to the Supreme Court.

The Supreme Court stated that, because Scott, as a slave, was not a US citizen, his time in free states did not change his status. He also did not have the right to sue. In addition, the Court determined that the Missouri Compromise was unconstitutional, stating that Congress had overstepped its bounds by outlawing slavery in the territories.

> ➤ **Review Video:** Dred Scott Act
> *Visit **mometrix.com/academy** and enter **Code**: **448931***

Harper's Ferry and John Brown

John Brown, an abolitionist, had participated in several anti-slavery activities, including killing five pro-slavery men in retaliation, after the sacking of Lawrence, Kansas, an anti-slavery town. He and other abolitionists also banded together to pool their funds and build a runaway slave colony.

In 1859, Brown seized a federal arsenal in Harper's Ferry, located in what is now West Virginia. Brown intended to seize guns and ammunition and lead a slave rebellion. Robert E. Lee captured Brown and 21 followers, who were subsequently tried and hanged. While Northerners took the executions as an indication that the government supported slavery, Southerners were of the opinion that most of the North supported Brown and were, in general, anti-slavery.

1860 election

The 1860 Presidential candidates represented four different parties, each with a different opinion on slavery:
- John Breckinridge, representing the Southern Democrats, was pro-slavery but urged compromise to preserve the Union.
- Abraham Lincoln, of the Republican Party, was anti-slavery.
- Stephen Douglas, of the Northern Democrats, felt that the issue should be determined locally, on a state-by-state basis.
- John Bell, of the Constitutional Union Party, focused primarily on keeping the Union intact.

In the end, Abraham Lincoln won both the popular and electoral election. Southern states, who had sworn to secede from the Union if Lincoln was elected did so, led by South Carolina. Shortly thereafter, the Civil War began when Confederate shots were fired on Fort Sumter in Charleston.

Advantages of the North and South in the Civil War

The Northern states had significant advantages, including:
- Larger population—the North consisted of 24 states while the South had 11.
- Better transportation and finances—with railroads primarily in the North, supply chains were much more dependable, as was overseas trade.
- Raw materials—the North held the majority of America's gold, as well as iron, copper, and other minerals vital to wartime.

The South's advantages included:
- Better-trained military officers—many of the Southern officers were West Point trained and had commanded in the Mexican and Indian wars.
- Familiarity with weapons—the climate and lifestyle of the South meant most of the people were experienced with both guns and horses. The industrial North had less extensive experience.
- Defensive position—the South felt that victory was guaranteed, since they were protecting their own lands, while the North would be invading.
- Well-defined goals—the South fought an ideological war to be allowed to govern themselves and preserve their way of life. The North originally fought to preserve the Union and later to free the slaves.

Emancipation Proclamation

The Emancipation Proclamation, issued by President Lincoln on January 1, 1863, freed all slaves in Confederate states that were still in rebellion against the Union. While the original proclamation did not free any slaves in the states actually under Union control, it did set a precedent for the emancipation of slaves as the war progressed.

The Emancipation Proclamation worked in the Union's favor as many freed slaves and other black troops joined the Union Army. Almost 200,000 blacks fought in the Union army, and over 10,000 served in the navy. By the end of the war, over 4 million slaves had been freed, and in 1865 slavery was abolished in the 13th amendment to the Constitution.

> ➤ **Review Video:** Emancipation Proclamation
> *Visit **mometrix.com/academy** and enter **Code: 511675***

Civil War events

Six major events of the Civil War and their outcomes or significance are:
- The First Battle of Bull Run (July 21, 1861)—this was the first major land battle of the war. Observers, expecting to enjoy an entertaining skirmish, set up picnics nearby. Instead, they found themselves witness to a bloodbath. Union forces were defeated, and the battle set the course of the Civil War as long, bloody and costly.
- The Capture of Fort Henry by Ulysses S. Grant—this battle in February of 1862 marked the Union's first major victory.
- The Battle of Gettysburg (July 1-3, 1863)—often seen as the turning point of the war, Gettysburg also saw the largest number of casualties of the war, with over 50,000 dead, wounded, or missing. Robert E. Lee was defeated, and the Confederate army, significantly crippled, withdrew.

- The Overland Campaign (May and June of 1864)—Grant, now in command of all the Union armies, led this high casualty campaign that eventually positioned the Union for victory.
- Sherman's March to the Sea—William Tecumseh Sherman, in May of 1864, conquered Atlanta. He then continued to Savannah, destroying vast amounts of property as he went.
- Following Lee's defeat at the Appomattox Courthouse, General Grant accepted Lee's surrender in the home of Wilmer McLean in Appomattox, Virginia on April 9, 1865.

Lincoln's assassination

The Civil War ended with the surrender of the South on April 9, 1865. Five days later, Lincoln and his wife, Mary, attended the play *Our American Cousin* at the Ford Theater. John Wilkes Booth performed his part in a conspiracy to aid the Confederacy by shooting Lincoln in the back of the head. Booth was tracked down and killed by Union soldiers 12 days later. Lincoln, carried from the theater to a nearby house, died the next morning.

Reconstruction and the Freedmen's Bureau

In the aftermath of the Civil War, the South was left in chaos. From 1865 to 1877, government on all levels worked to help restore order to the South, ensure civil rights to the freed slaves, and bring the Confederate states back into the Union. This became known as the Reconstruction period. In 1866, Congress passed the Reconstruction Acts, placing former Confederate states under military rule and stating the grounds for readmission into the Union.

The Freedmen's Bureau was formed to help freedmen both with basic necessities like food and clothing and also with employment and finding of family members who had been separated during the war. Many in the South felt the Freedmen's Bureau worked to set freed slaves against their former owners. The Bureau was intended to help former slaves become self-sufficient, and to keep them from falling prey to those who would take advantage of them. It eventually closed due to lack of funding and to violence from the Ku Klux Klan.

Radical and Moderate Republicans

The Radical Republicans wished to treat the South quite harshly after the war. Thaddeus Stevens, the House Leader, suggested that the Confederate states be treated as if they were territories again, with ten years of military rule and territorial government before they would be readmitted. He also wanted to give all black men the right to vote. Former Confederate soldiers would be required to swear they had never supported the Confederacy (knows as the "Ironclad Oath") in order to be granted full rights as American citizens.

In contrast, the moderate Republicans wanted only black men who were literate or who had served as Union troops to be able to vote. All Confederate soldiers except troop leaders would also be able to vote. Before his death, Lincoln had favored a more moderate approach to Reconstruction, hoping this approach might bring some states back into the Union before the end of the war.

Black Codes, the Civil Rights Act, and impeachment of Andrew Johnson

The Black Codes were proposed to control freed slaves. They would not be allowed to bear arms, assemble, serve on juries, or testify against whites. Schools would be segregated, and unemployed blacks could be arrested and forced to work. The Civil Rights Act countered these codes, providing much wider rights for the freed slaves. Andrew Johnson, who became president after Lincoln's death, supported the Black Codes and vetoed the Civil Rights Act in 1865 and again in 1866. The second time, Congress overrode his veto and it became law. Two years later, Congress voted to impeach Johnson, the culmination of tensions between Congress and the president. He was tried and came within a single vote of being convicted, but ultimately was acquitted and finished his term in office.

Thirteenth, Fourteenth and Fifteenth Amendments

The Thirteenth, Fourteenth and Fifteenth Amendments were all passed shortly after the end of the Civil War:
- The Thirteenth Amendment was ratified by the states on December 6, 1865. This amendment prohibited slavery in the United States.
- The Fourteenth Amendment overturned the Dred Scott decision, and was ratified July 9, 1868. American citizenship was redefined: a citizen was any person born or naturalized in the US, with all citizens guaranteed equal protection by all states. It also guaranteed citizens of any race the right to file a lawsuit or serve on a jury.
- The Fifteenth Amendment was ratified February 3, 1870. It states that no citizen of the United States can be denied the right to vote based on race, color, or previous status as a slave.

> ➤ **Review Video:** The 13th Amendment
> Visit **mometrix.com/academy** and enter **Code: 867407**

> ➤ **Review Video:** The 14th Amendment
> Visit **mometrix.com/academy** and enter **Code: 928755**

> ➤ **Review Video:** The 15th Amendment
> Visit **mometrix.com/academy** and enter **Code: 102009**

Reconstruction

The three phases of Reconstruction are:
- Presidential Reconstruction—largely driven by President Andrew Johnson's policies, the Presidential phase of Reconstruction was lenient on the South and allowed continued discrimination against and control over blacks.
- Congressional Reconstruction—Congress, controlled largely by Radical Republicans, took a different stance, providing a wider range of civil rights for blacks and greater control over Southern government. Congressional Reconstruction is marked by military control of the former Confederate States.
- Redemption—gradually, the Confederate states were readmitted into the union. During this time, white Democrats took over the government of most of the South. In 1877, President Rutherford Hayes withdrew the last federal troops from the South.

Carpetbaggers and Scalawags

The chaos in the south attracted a number of people seeking to fill the power vacuums and take advantage of the economic disruption. Scalawags were southern Whites who aligned with Freedmen to take over local governments. Many in the South who could have filled political offices refused to take the necessary oath required to grant them the right to vote, leaving many opportunities for Scalawags and others. Carpetbaggers were northerners who traveled to the South for various reasons. Some provided assistance, while others sought to make money or to acquire political power during this chaotic period.

Transcontinental railroad

In 1869, the Union Pacific Railroad completed the first section of a planned transcontinental railroad. This section went from Omaha, Nebraska to Sacramento, California. Ninety percent of the workers were Chinese, working in very dangerous conditions for very low pay. With the rise of the railroad, products were much more easily transported across the country. While this was positive overall for industry throughout the country, it was often damaging to family farmers, who found themselves paying high shipping costs for smaller supply orders while larger companies received major discounts.

Immigration limits

In 1870, the Naturalization Act put limits on US citizenship, allowing full citizenship only to whites and those of African descent. The Chinese Exclusion Act of 1882 put limits on Chinese immigration. The Immigration Act of 1882 taxed immigrants, charging fifty cents per person. These funds helped pay administrative costs for regulating immigration. Ellis Island opened in 1892 as a processing center for those arriving in New York. 1921 saw the Emergency Quota Act passed, also known as the Johnson Quota Act, which severely limited the number of immigrants allowed into the country.

Nineteenth century changes in agriculture

Technological advancements
During the mid 1800s, irrigation techniques improved significantly. Advances occurred in cultivation and breeding, as well as fertilizer use and crop rotation. In the Great Plains, also known as the Great American Desert, the dense soil was finally cultivated with steel plows. In 1892, gasoline-powered tractors arrived, and were widely used by 1900. Other advancements in agriculture's toolset included barbed wire fences, combines, silos, deep-water wells, and the cream separator.

Government actions
Four major government actions that helped improve US agriculture in the nineteenth century are:
- The Department of Agriculture came into being in 1862, working for the interests of farmers and ranchers across the country.
- The Morrill Land-Grant Acts were a series of acts passed between 1862 and 1890, allowing land-grant colleges.
- In conjunction with land-grant colleges, the Hatch Act of 1887 brought agriculture experiment stations into the picture, helping discover new farming techniques.

- In 1914, the Smith-Lever Act provided cooperative programs to help educate people about food, home economics, community development and agriculture. Related agriculture extension programs helped farmers increase crop production to feed the rapidly growing nation.

Inventors and inventions

Major inventors from the 1800s and their inventions are:
- Alexander Graham Bell—the telephone
- Orville and Wilbur Wright—the airplane
- Richard Gatling—the machine gun
- Walter Hunt, Elias Howe and Isaac Singer—the sewing machine
- Nikola Tesla—alternating current
- George Eastman—the Kodak camera
- Thomas Edison—light bulbs, motion pictures, the phonograph
- Samuel Morse—the telegraph
- Charles Goodyear—vulcanized rubber
- Cyrus McCormick—the reaper
- George Westinghouse—the transformer, the air brake

This was an active period for invention, with about 700,000 patents registered between 1860 and 1900.

Gilded Age

The time period from the end of the Civil War to the beginning of the First World War is often referred to as the Gilded Age, or the Second Industrial Revolution. The US was changing from an agricultural-based economy to an industrial economy, with rapid growth accompanying the shift. In addition, the country itself was expanding, spreading into the seemingly unlimited West. This time period saw the beginning of banks, department stores, chain stores, and trusts—all familiar features of the modern-day landscape. Cities also grew rapidly, and large numbers of immigrants arrived in the country, swelling the urban ranks.

> **Review Video:** The Gilded Age: An Overview
> *Visit **mometrix.com/academy** and enter **Code**: **684770***

Populist Party

A major recession struck the United States during the 1890s, with crop prices falling dramatically. Drought compounded the problems, leaving many American farmers in crippling debt. The Farmers' Alliance formed in 1875, drawing the rural poor into a single political entity.

Recession also affected the more industrial parts of the country. The Knights of Labor, formed in 1869 by Uriah Stephens, was able to unite workers into a union to protect their rights. Dissatisfied by views espoused by industrialists, these two groups, the Farmers Alliance and the Knights of Labor, joined to form the Populist Party, also known as the People's Party, in 1892. Some of the elements of the party's platform included:

- National currency
- Graduated income tax
- Government ownership of railroads as well as telegraph and telephone systems
- Secret ballots for voting
- Immigration restriction
- Single-term limits for President and Vice-President

The Populist Party was in favor of decreasing elitism and making the voice of the common man more easily heard in the political process.

Labor movement

One of the first large, well-organized strikes occurred in 1892. Called the Homestead Strike, it occurred when the Amalgamated Association of Iron and Steel Workers struck against the Carnegie Steel Company. Gunfire ensued, and Carnegie was able to eliminate the plant's union. In 1894, workers in the American Railway Union, led by Eugene Debs, initiated the Pullman Strike after the Pullman Palace Car Co. cut their wages by 28 percent. President Grover Cleveland called in troops to break up the strike on the grounds that it interfered with mail delivery. Mary Harris "Mother" Jones organized the Children's Crusade to protest child labor. A protest march proceeded to the home of President Theodore Roosevelt in 1903. Jones also worked with the United Mine Workers of America, and helped found the Industrial Workers of the World.

> **Review Video:** The Gilded Age: Labor Strikes
> *Visit **mometrix.com/academy** and enter **Code**: 683116*

> **Review Video:** The Gilded Age: Labor Unions
> *Visit **mometrix.com/academy** and enter **Code**: 749692*

Panic of 1893

Far from a US-centric event, the Panic of 1893 was an economic crisis that affected most of the globe. As a response, President Grover Cleveland repealed the Sherman Silver Purchase Act, afraid it had caused the downturn rather than boosting the economy as intended. The Panic led to bankruptcies, with banks and railroads going under and factory unemployment rising as high as 25 percent. In the end, the Republican Party regained power due to the economic crisis.

Progressive Era

From the 1890s to the end of the First World War, Progressives set forth an ideology that drove many levels of society and politics. The Progressives were in favor of workers' rights and safety, and wanted measures taken against waste and corruption. They felt science could help improve society, and that the government could—and should—provide answers to a variety of social problems. Progressives came from a wide variety of backgrounds, but were united in their desire to improve society.

<u>Muckrakers</u>
"Muckrakers" was a term used to identify aggressive investigative journalists who exposed scandals, corruption, and many other wrongs in late nineteenth century society. Among these intrepid writers were:
- Ida Tarbell—she exposed John D. Rockefeller's Standard Oil Trust.
- Jacob Riis—a photographer, he brought the living conditions of the poor in New York to the public's attention.
- Lincoln Steffens—he worked to expose political corruption in municipal government.
- Upton Sinclair—his book *The Jungle* led to reforms in the meat-packing industry.

Through the work of these journalists, many new policies came into being, including workmen's compensation, child labor laws, and trust-busting.

<u>Sixteenth, Seventeenth, Eighteenth and Nineteenth Amendments</u>
The early twentieth century saw several amendments made to the US Constitution:
- The Sixteenth Amendment (1913) established a federal income tax.
- The Seventeenth Amendment (1913) allowed popular election of senators.
- The Eighteenth Amendment (1919) prohibited the sale, production and transportation of alcohol. This amendment was later repealed by the Twenty-first Amendment.
- The Nineteenth Amendment (1920) gave women the right to vote.

These amendments largely grew out of the Progressive Era, as many citizens worked to improve American society.

<u>Federal Trade Commission and elimination of trusts</u>
Muckrakers such as Ida Tarbell and Lincoln Steffens brought to light the damaging trend of trusts—huge corporations working to monopolize areas of commerce so they could control prices and distribution. The Sherman Antitrust Act and the Clayton Antitrust Act set out guidelines for competition among corporations and set out to eliminate these trusts. The Federal Trade Commission was formed in 1914 in order to enforce antitrust measures and ensure that companies were operated fairly and did not create controlling monopolies.

> ➤ **Review Video:** The Progressive Era
> *Visit **mometrix.com/academy** and enter **Code**: 293582*

Government dealings with Native Americans

America's westward expansion led to conflict and violent confrontations with Native Americans such as the Battle of Little Bighorn. In 1876, the American government ordered all Indians to relocate to reservations. Lack of compliance led to the Dawes Act in 1887, which ordered assimilation rather than separation: Native Americans were offered American citizenship and a piece of their tribal land if they would accept the lot chosen by the government and live on it separately from the tribe. This act remained in effect until 1934. Reformers also forced Indian children to attend Indian Boarding Schools, where they were not allowed to speak their native language and were immersed into a Euro-American culture and religion. Children were often abused in these schools, and were indoctrinated to abandon their identity as Native Americans. In 1890, the massacre at Wounded Knee, accompanied by Geronimo's surrender, led the Native Americans to work to preserve their culture rather than fight for their lands.

<u>Native Americans in wartime</u>
The Spanish-American war (1898) saw a number of Native Americans serving with Teddy Roosevelt in the Rough Riders. Apache scouts accompanied General John J. Pershing to Mexico, hoping to find Pancho Villa. More than 17,000 Native Americans were drafted into service for World War I, though at the time they were not considered legal citizens. In 1924, Indians were finally granted official citizenship by the Indian Citizenship Act.

After decades of relocation, forced assimilation, and genocide, the number of Native Americans in the US has greatly declined. Though many Native Americans have chosen—or have been forced—to assimilate, about 300 reservations exist today, with most of their inhabitants living in abject poverty.

Spanish-American War

Spain had controlled Cuba since the fifteenth century. Over the centuries, the Spanish had quashed a variety of revolts. In 1886, slavery ended in Cuba, and another revolt was rising. In the meantime, the US had expressed interest in Cuba, offering Spain $130 million for the island in 1853, during Franklin Pierce's presidency. In 1898, the Cuban revolt was underway. In spite of various factions supporting the Cubans, the US President, William McKinley, refused to recognize the rebellion, preferring negotiation over involvement in war. Then the *Maine*, a US battleship in Havana Harbor, was blown up, killing 266 crew members. The US declared war two months later, and the war ended with a Spanish surrender in less than four months.

Panama Canal

Initial work began on the Panama Canal in 1881, though the idea had been discussed since the 1500s. The canal greatly reduces the length and time needed to sail from one ocean to the other by connecting the Atlantic to the Pacific through the Isthmus of Panama, which joins South America to North America. Before the canal was built, travelers had to sail around the entire perimeter of South America to reach the West Coast of the US. The French began the work after successfully completing the Suez Canal, which connected the Mediterranean Sea to the Red Sea. However, due to disease and high expense the work moved slowly and after eight years the company went bankrupt, suspending work. The US purchased the holdings, and the first ship sailed through the canal in 1914. The Panama Canal was constructed as a lock-and-lake canal, with ships lifted on locks to travel from one lake to another over the rugged, mountainous terrain. In order to maintain control of the Canal Zone, the US assisted Panama in its battle for independence from Columbia.

Roosevelt's "Big Stick Diplomacy" and foreign policy in South America

Theodore Roosevelt's famous quote, "Speak softly and carry a big stick," is supposedly of African origins, at least according to Roosevelt. He used this proverb to justify expanded involvement in foreign affairs during his tenure as President. The US military was deployed to protect American interests in Latin America. Roosevelt also worked to maintain an equal or greater influence in Latin America than those held by European interests. As a result, the US Navy grew larger, and the US generally became more involved in foreign affairs. Roosevelt felt that if any country was left vulnerable to control by Europe, due to economic issues or political instability, the US had not only a right to intervene, but was obligated to do so. This led to US involvement in Cuba, Nicaragua, Haiti and the Dominican Republic over several decades leading into the First and Second World Wars.

William Howard Taft's "Dollar Diplomacy"

During William Howard Taft's presidency, Taft instituted "Dollar Diplomacy." This approach was America's effort to influence Latin America and East Asia through economic rather than military means. Taft saw past efforts in these areas to be political and warlike, while his efforts focused on peaceful economic goals. His justification of the policy was to protect the Panama Canal, which was vital to US trade interests.

In spite of Taft's assurance that Dollar Diplomacy was a peaceful approach, many interventions proved violent. During Latin American revolts, such as those in Nicaragua, the US sent troops to settle the revolutions. Afterwards, bankers moved in to help support the new leaders through loans. Dollar Diplomacy continued until 1913, when Woodrow Wilson was elected President.

Woodrow Wilson's "Moral Diplomacy"

Turning away from Taft's "Dollar Diplomacy," Wilson instituted a foreign policy he referred to as "moral diplomacy." This approach still influences American foreign policy today. Wilson felt that representative government and democracy in all countries would lead to worldwide stability. Democratic governments, he felt, would be less likely to threaten American interests. He also saw the US and Great Britain as the great role models in this area, as well as champions of world peace and self-government. Free trade and international commerce would allow the US to speak out regarding world events. Main elements of Wilson's policies included:
- Maintaining a strong military
- Promoting democracy throughout the world
- Expanding international trade to boost the American economy

First World War

World War I occurred from 1914 to 1918 and was fought largely in Europe. Triggered by the assassination of Austrian Archduke Franz Ferdinand, the war rapidly escalated. At the beginning of the conflict, Woodrow Wilson declared the US neutral. Major events influencing US involvement included:
- Sinking of the *Lusitania*—the British passenger liner RMS *Lusitania* was sunk by a German U-boat in 1915. Among the 1,000 civilian victims were over 100 American citizens. Outraged by this act, many Americans began to push for US involvement in the war, using the *Lusitania* as a rallying cry.
- German U-boat aggression—Wilson continued to keep the US out of the war, using as his 1916 reelection slogan, "He kept us out of war." While he continued to work toward an end of the war, German U-boats began to indiscriminately attack

American and Canadian merchant ships carrying supplies to Germany's enemies in Europe.

- Zimmerman Telegram —the final event that brought the US into World War I was the interception of the Zimmerman Telegram (also known as the Zimmerman Note). In this telegram, Germany proposed forming an alliance with the Mexico if the US entered the war.

> ➢ **Review Video:** World War I: An Overview
> *Visit **mometrix.com/academy** and enter **Code**: 994468*

US efforts during World War I

American railroads came under government control in December 1917. The widespread system was consolidated into a single system, with each region assigned a director. This greatly increased the efficiency of the railroad system, allowing the railroads to supply both domestic and military needs. Control returned to private ownership in 1920. In 1918, telegraph, telephone and cable services also came under Federal control, to be returned to private management the next year. The American Red Cross supported the war effort by knitting clothes for Army and Navy troops. They also helped supply hospital and refugee clothing and surgical dressings. Over eight million people participated in this effort. To generate wartime funds, the US government sold Liberty Bonds. In four issues, they sold nearly $25 billion—more than one fifth of Americans purchased them. After the war, a fifth bond drive was held, but sold "Victory Liberty Bonds."

Wilson's Fourteen Points

President Woodrow Wilson proposed Fourteen Points as the basis for a peace settlement to end the war. Presented to the US Congress in January 1918, the Fourteen Points included:
- Five points outlining general ideals
- Eight points to resolve immediate problems of political and territorial nature
- One point proposing an organization of nations (the League of Nations) with the intent of maintaining world peace

In November of that same year, Germany agreed to an armistice, assuming the final treaty would be based on the Fourteen Points. However, during the peace conference in Paris 1919, there was much disagreement, leading to a final agreement that punished Germany and the other Central Powers much more than originally intended. Henry Cabot Lodge, who had become the Foreign Relations Committee chairman in 1918, wanted an unconditional surrender from Germany and was concerned about the article in the Treaty of Versailles that gave the League of Nations power to declare war without a vote from the US Congress. A League of Nations was included in the Treaty of Versailles at Wilson's insistence. The Senate rejected the Treaty of Versailles, and in the end Wilson refused to concede to Lodge's demands. As a result, the US did not join the League of Nations.

> ➢ **Review Video:** Woodrow Wilson's Fourteen Points
> *Visit **mometrix.com/academy** and enter **Code**: 335789*

America during the 1920s

The post-war 1920s saw many Americans moving from the farm to the city, with growing prosperity in the US. The Roaring Twenties, or the Jazz Age, was driven largely by growth in the automobile and entertainment industries. Individuals like Charles Lindbergh, the first aviator to make a solo flight cross the Atlantic Ocean, added to the American admiration of individual accomplishment. Telephone lines, distribution of electricity, highways, the radio, and other inventions brought great changes to everyday life.

African-American cultural movements

The Harlem Renaissance saw a number of African-American artists settling in Harlem in New York. This community produced a number of well-known artists and writers, including Langston Hughes, Nella Larsen, Zora Neale Hurston, Claude McKay, Countee Cullen and Jean Toomer. The growth of jazz, also largely driven by African Americans, defined the Jazz Age. Its unconventional, improvisational style matched the growing sense of optimism and exploration of the decade. Originating as an offshoot of the blues, jazz began in New Orleans. Some significant jazz musicians were Duke Ellington, Louis Armstrong and Jelly Roll Morton. Big Band and Swing Jazz also developed in the 1920s. Well-known musicians of this movement included Bing Crosby, Frank Sinatra, Count Basie, Benny Goodman, Billie Holiday, Ella Fitzgerald and The Dorsey Brothers.

National Origins Act of 1924

The National Origins Act (Johnson-Reed Act) placed limitations on immigration. The number of immigrants allowed into the US was based on the population of each nationality of immigrants who were living in the country in 1890. Only two percent of each nationality's 1890 population numbers were allowed to immigrate. This led to great disparities between immigrants from various nations, and Asian immigration was not allowed at all. Some of the impetus behind the Johnson-Reed Act came as a result of paranoia following the Russian Revolution. Fear of communist influences in the US led to a general fear of immigrants.

Red Scare

World War I created many jobs, but after the war ended these jobs disappeared, leaving many unemployed. In the wake of these employment changes the International Workers of the World and the Socialist Party, headed by Eugene Debs, became more and more visible. Workers initiated strikes in an attempt to regain the favorable working conditions that had been put into place before the war. Unfortunately, many of these strikes became violent, and the actions were blamed on "Reds," or Communists, for trying to spread their views into America. With the recent Bolshevik Revolution in Russia, many Americans feared a similar revolution might occur in the US. The Red Scare ensued, with many individuals jailed for supposedly holding communist, anarchist or socialist beliefs.

Growth of civil rights for African-Americans

Marcus Garvey founded the Universal Negro Improvement Association and African Communities League (UNIA-ACL), which became a large and active organization focused on building black nationalism. In 1909, the National Association for the Advancement of Colored People (NAACP) came into being, working to defeat Jim Crow laws. The NAACP also helped prevent racial segregation from becoming federal law, fought against lynchings, helped black soldiers in WWI become officers, and helped defend the Scottsboro Boys, who were unjustly accused of rape.

Ku Klux Klan

In 1866, Confederate Army veterans came together to fight against Reconstruction in the South, forming a group called the Ku Klux Klan (KKK). With white supremacist beliefs, including anti-Semitism, nativism, anti-Catholicism, and overt racism, this organization relied heavily on violence to get its message across. In 1915, they grew again in power, using a film called *The Birth of a Nation*, by D.W. Griffith, to spread their ideas. In the 1920s, the reach of the KKK spread far into the North and Midwest, and members controlled a number of state governments. Its membership and power began to decline during the Great Depression, but experienced a resurgence later.

American Civil Liberties Union

The American Civil Liberties Union (ACLU), founded in 1920, grew from the American Union Against Militarism. The ACLU helped conscientious objectors avoid going to war during WWI, and also helped those being prosecuted under the Espionage Act (1917) and the Sedition Act (1918), many of whom were immigrants. Their major goals were to protect immigrants and other citizens who were threatened with prosecution for their political beliefs, and to support labor unions, which were also under threat by the government during the Red Scare.

Anti-Defamation League

In 1913, the Anti-Defamation League was formed to prevent anti-Semitic behavior and practices. Its actions also worked to prevent all forms of racism, and to prevent individuals from being discriminated against for any reason involving their race. They spoke against the Ku Klux Klan, as well as other racist or anti-Semitic organizations. This organization still works to fight discrimination against all minorities.

Great Depression

The Great Depression, which began in 1929 with the stock market crash, grew out of several factors that had developed over the previous years including:
- Growing economic disparity between the rich and middle classes, with the rich amassing wealth much more quickly than the lower classes
- Disparity in economic distribution in industries
- Growing use of credit, leading to an inflated demand for some goods
- Government support of new industries rather than agriculture
- Risky stock market investments, leading to the stock market crash

Additional factors contributing to the Depression also included the Labor Day Hurricane in the Florida Keys (1935) and the Great Hurricane of 1938 in New England, along with the Dust Bowl in the Great Plains, which destroyed crops and resulted in the displacement of as many as 2.5 million people.

> ➤ **Review Video:** The Great Depression
> *Visit **mometrix.com/academy** and enter **Code**: **331401**

Roosevelt administration

Roosevelt's "New Deal"
Franklin D. Roosevelt was elected president in 1932 with his promise of a "New Deal" for Americans. His goals were to provide government work programs to provide jobs, wages and relief to numerous workers throughout the beleaguered US. Congress gave Roosevelt almost free rein to produce relief legislation. The goals of this legislation were:
- Relief—creating jobs for the high numbers of unemployed
- Recovery—stimulating the economy through the National Recovery Administration
- Reform—passing legislation to prevent future, similar economic crashes

The Roosevelt Administration also passed legislation regarding ecological issues, including the Soil Conservation Service, aimed at preventing another Dust Bowl.

Roosevelt's "alphabet organizations"
So-called "alphabet organizations" set up during Roosevelt's administration included:
- Civilian Conservation Corps (CCC)—provided jobs in the forestry service
- Agricultural Adjustment Administration (AAA)—increased agricultural income by adjusting both production and prices
- Tennessee Valley Authority (TVA)—organized projects to build dams in the Tennessee River for flood control and production of electricity, resulting in increased productivity for industries in the area, and easier navigation of the Tennessee River
- Public Works Administration (PWA) and Civil Works Administration (CWA)—provided a multitude of jobs, initiating over 34,000 projects
- Works Progress Administration (WPA)—helped unemployed persons to secure employment on government work projects or elsewhere

Actions taken to prevent future crashes and stabilize the economy
The Roosevelt administration passed several laws and established several institutions to initiate the "reform" portion of the New Deal, including:
- Glass-Steagall Act—separated investment from commercial banking
- Securities Exchange Commission (SEC)—helped regulate Wall Street investment practices, making them less dangerous to the overall economy
- Wagner Act—provided worker and union rights to improve relations between employees and employers
- Social Security Act of 1935—provided pensions as well as unemployment insurance

Other actions focused on insuring bank deposits and adjusting the value of American currency. Most of these regulatory agencies and government policies and programs still exist today.

Labor regulations

Three major regulations regarding labor that were passed after the Great Depression are:
- The Wagner Act (1935)—also known as the National Labor Relations Act, it established that unions were legal, protected members of unions, and required collective bargaining. This act was later amended by the Taft-Hartley Act of 1947 and the Landrum-Griffin Act of 1959, which further clarified certain elements.
- Davis-Bacon Act (1931)—provided fair compensation for contractors and subcontractors
- Walsh-Healey Act (1936)—established a minimum wage, child labor laws, safety standards, and overtime pay

World War II

Interventionist and Isolationist approaches to involvement
When war broke out in Europe in 1939, President Roosevelt stated that the US would remain neutral. However, his overall approach was considered "interventionist," as he was willing to provide aid to the Allies without actually entering the conflict. Thus the US supplied a wide variety of war materials to the Allied nations in the early years of the war.

Isolationists believed the US should not provide any aid to the Allies, including supplies. They felt Roosevelt, by assisting the Allies, was leading the US into a war for which it was not prepared. Led by Charles Lindbergh, the Isolationists believed that any involvement in the European conflict endangered the US by weakening its national defense.

> **Review Video:** World War II: An Overview
> *Visit **mometrix.com/academy** and enter **Code**: **254317***

US entry into the war
In 1937, Japan invaded China, prompting the US to eventually halt exports to Japan. Roosevelt also did not allow Japanese interests to withdraw money held in US banks. In 1941, General Tojo rose to power as the Japanese prime minister. Recognizing America's ability to bring a halt to Japan's expansion, he authorized the bombing of Pearl Harbor on December 7. The US responded by declaring war on Japan. Partially because of the Tripartite Pact among the Axis Powers, Germany and Italy then declared war on the US, later followed by Bulgaria, Hungary, and other Axis nations.

Surrender of Germany
In 1941, Hitler violated the non-aggression pact he had signed with Stalin two years earlier by invading the USSR. Stalin then joined the Allies. Stalin, Roosevelt and Winston Churchill planned to defeat Germany first, then Japan, bringing the war to an end.

In 1942-1943, the Allies drove Axis forces out of Africa. In addition, the Germans were soundly defeated at Stalingrad.

The Italian Campaign involved Allied operations in Italy between July 1943 and May 1945, including Italy's liberation. On June 6, 1944, known as D-Day, the Allies invaded France at Normandy. Soviet troops moved on the eastern front at the same time, driving German

- 34 -

forces back. By April 25, 1945, Berlin was surrounded by Soviet troops. On May 7, Germany surrendered.

> ➤ **Review Video:** <u>World War II: Germany</u>
> *Visit **mometrix.com/academy** and enter **Code**: **951452**

Surrender of Japan

War continued with Japan after Germany's surrender. Japanese forces had taken a large portion of Southeast Asia and the Western Pacific, all the way to the Aleutian Islands in Alaska. General Doolittle bombed several Japanese cities while American troops scored a victory at Midway. Additional fighting in the Battle of the Coral Sea further weakened Japan's position. As a final blow, the US dropped two atomic bombs on Japan, one on Hiroshima and the other on Nagasaki. This was the first time atomic bombs had been used in warfare, and the devastation was horrific and demoralizing. Japan surrendered on September 2, 1945, which became V-J Day in the US.

> ➤ **Review Video:** <u>World War II: Japan</u>
> *Visit **mometrix.com/academy** and enter **Code**: **313104**

442nd Regimental Combat Team, the Tuskegee Airmen, and the Navajo Code Talkers

The 442nd Regimental Combat Team consisted of Japanese-Americans fighting in Europe for the US. The most highly decorated unit per member in US history, they suffered a 93% casualty rate during the war. The Tuskegee Airmen were African-American aviators, the first black Americans allowed to fly for the military. In spite of being ineligible to become official navy pilots, they flew over 15,000 missions and were highly decorated. The Navajo Code Talkers were native Navajo who used their traditional language to transmit information among Allied forces. Because Navajo is a language and not simply a code, the Axis powers were never able to translate it. Use of Navajo Code Talkers to transmit information was instrumental in the taking of Iwo Jima and other major victories of the war.

Women during World War II

Women served widely in the military during WWII, working in numerous positions, including the Flight Nurses Corps. Women also moved into the workforce while men were overseas, leading to over 19 million women in the US workforce by 1944. Rosie the Riveter stood as a symbol of these women and a means of recruiting others to take needed positions. Women, as well as their families left behind during wartime, also grew Victory Gardens to help provide food.

Atomic bomb

The atomic bomb, developed during WWII, was the most powerful bomb ever invented. A single bomb, carried by a single plane, held enough power to destroy an entire city. This devastating effect was demonstrated with the bombing of Hiroshima and Nagasaki in 1945 in what later became a controversial move, but ended the war. The bombings resulted in as many as 150,000 immediate deaths and many more as time passed after the bombings, mostly due to radiation poisoning.

Whatever the arguments against the use of "The Bomb," the post WWII era saw many countries develop similar weapons to match the newly expanded military power of the US.

The impact of those developments and use of nuclear weapons continues to haunt international relations today.

Yalta Conference and the Potsdam Conference

In February 1945, Joseph Stalin, Franklin D. Roosevelt and Winston Churchill met in Yalta to discuss the post-war treatment of the Axis nations, particularly Germany. Though Germany had not yet surrendered, its defeat was imminent. After Germany's official surrender, Joseph Stalin, Harry Truman (Roosevelt's successor), and Clement Attlee (replacing Churchill partway through the conference) met to formalize those plans.

This meeting was called the Potsdam Conference. Basic provisions of these agreements included:
- Dividing Germany and Berlin into four zones of occupation
- Demilitarization of Germany
- Poland remaining under Soviet control
- Outlawing the Nazi Party
- Trials for Nazi leaders
- Relocation of numerous German citizens
- The USSR joining the United Nations, established in 1945
- Establishment of the United Nations Security Council, consisting of the US, the UK, the USSR, China and France

Agreements made with post-war Japan

General Douglas MacArthur led the American military occupation of Japan after the country surrendered. The goals of the US occupation included removing Japan's military and making the country a democracy. A 1947 constitution removed power from the emperor and gave it to the people, as well as granting voting rights to women. Japan was no longer allowed to declare war, and a group of 28 government officials were tried for war crimes. In 1951, the US finally signed a peace treaty with Japan. This treaty allowed Japan to rearm itself for purposes of self-defense, but stripped the country of the empire it had built overseas.

Alien Registration Act and treatment of Japanese immigrants

In 1940, the US passed the Alien Registration Act, which required all aliens older than fourteen to be fingerprinted and registered. They were also required to report changes of address within five days.

Tension between whites and Japanese immigrants in California, which had been building since the beginning of the century, came to a head with the bombing of Pearl Harbor in 1941. Believing that even those Japanese living in the US were likely to be loyal to their native country, the president ordered numerous Japanese to be arrested on suspicion of subversive action and isolated in exclusion zones known as War Relocation Camps. Approximately 120,000 Japanese-Americans, two-thirds of them US citizens, were sent to these camps during the war.

General state of the US after World War II

Following WWII, the US became the strongest political power in the world, becoming a major player in world affairs and foreign policies. The US determined to stop the spread of communism, having named itself the "arsenal of democracy" during the war. In addition, America emerged with a greater sense of itself as a single, integrated nation, with many regional and economic differences diminished. The government worked for greater equality and the growth of communications increased contact among different areas of the country. Both the aftermath of the Great Depression and the necessities of WWII had given the government greater control over various institutions as well as the economy. This also meant that the American government took on greater responsibility for the well-being of its citizens, both in the domestic arena, such as providing basic needs, and in protecting them from foreign threats. This increased role of providing basic necessities for all Americans has been criticized by some as "the welfare state."

Harry S. Truman

Harry S. Truman took over the presidency from Franklin D. Roosevelt near the end of WWII. He made the final decision to drop atomic bombs on Japan and played a major role in the final decisions regarding treatment of post-war Germany. On the domestic front, Truman initiated a 21-point plan known as the Fair Deal. This plan expanded Social Security, provided public housing, and made the Fair Employment Practice Committee permanent. Truman helped support Greece and Turkey (which were under threat from the USSR), supported South Korea against communist North Korea, and helped with recovery in Western Europe. He also participated in the formation of NATO, the North Atlantic Treaty Organization.

Korean War

The Korean War began in 1950 and ended in 1953. For the first time in history, a world organization—the United Nations—played a military role in a war. North Korea sent communist troops into South Korea, seeking to bring the entire country under communist control. The UN sent out a call to member nations, asking them to support South Korea. Truman sent troops, as did many other UN member nations. The war ended three years later with a truce rather than a peace treaty, and Korea remains divided at the 38th parallel north, with communist rule remaining in the North and a democratic government ruling the South.

Dwight D. Eisenhower

Eisenhower carried out a middle-of-the-road foreign policy and brought the US several steps forward in equal rights. He worked to minimize tensions during the Cold War, and negotiated a peace treaty with Russia after the death of Stalin. He enforced desegregation by sending troops to Little Rock Central High School in Arkansas, as well as ordering the desegregation of the military. Organizations formed during his administration included the Department of Health, Education and Welfare, and the National Aeronautics and Space Administration (NASA).

John F. Kennedy

Although his term was cut short by his assassination, JFK instituted economic programs that led to a period of continuous expansion in the US unmatched since before WWII. He formed the Alliance for Progress and the Peace Corps, organizations intended to help developing nations. He also oversaw the passage of new civil rights legislation, and drafted plans to attack poverty and its causes, along with support of the arts. Kennedy's presidency ended when he was assassinated by Lee Harvey Oswald in 1963.

Cuban Missile Crisis

The Cuban Missile Crisis occurred in 1962, during John F. Kennedy's presidency. Russian Premier Nikita Khrushchev decided to place nuclear missiles in Cuba to protect the island from invasion by the US. An American U-2 plane flying over the island photographed the missile bases as they were being built. Tensions rose, with the US concerned about nuclear missiles so close to its shores, and the USSR concerned about American missiles that had been placed in Turkey. Eventually, the missile sites were removed, and a US naval blockade turned back Soviet ships carrying missiles to Cuba. During negotiations, the US agreed to remove their missiles from Turkey and agreed to sell surplus wheat to the USSR. A telephone hotline between Moscow and Washington was set up to allow instant communication between the two heads of state to prevent similar incidents in the future.

Lyndon B. Johnson

Kennedy's Vice President, Lyndon Johnson, assumed the presidency after Kennedy's assassination. He supported civil rights bills, tax cuts, and other wide-reaching legislation that Kennedy had also supported. Johnson saw America as a "Great Society," and enacted legislation to fight disease and poverty, renew urban areas, support education and environmental conservation. Medicare and Medicaid were instituted under his administration. He continued Kennedy's support of space exploration and he is also known, although less positively, for his handling of the Vietnam War.

Civil Rights Movement

In the 1950s, post-war America was experiencing a rapid growth in prosperity. However, African-Americans found themselves left behind. Following the lead of Mahatma Gandhi, who led similar class struggles in India, African-Americans began to demand equal rights. Major figures in this struggle included:
- Rosa Parks—often called the "mother of the Civil Rights Movement," her refusal to give up her seat on the bus to a white man served as a seed from which the movement grew.
- Martin Luther King, Jr.—the best-known leader of the movement, King drew on Gandhi's beliefs and encouraged non-violent opposition. He led a march on Washington in 1963, received the Nobel Peace Prize in 1964, and was assassinated in 1968.
- Malcolm X—espousing less peaceful means of change, Malcolm X became a Black Muslim, and supported black nationalism.
- Stokely Carmichael—Carmichael originated the term "Black Power" and served as head of the Student Nonviolent Coordinating Committee. He believed in black pride

and black culture, and felt separate political and social institutions should be developed for blacks.

- Adam Clayton Powell—chairman of the Coordinating Committee for Employment, he led rent strikes and other actions, as well as a bus boycott, to increase the hiring of blacks.
- Jesse Jackson—Jackson was selected to head the Chicago Operation Breadbasket in 1966, and went on to organize boycotts and other actions. He also had an unsuccessful run for President.

Three major events of the Civil Rights Movement are:

- Montgomery Bus Boycott—in 1955, Rosa Parks refused to give her seat on the bus to a white man. As a result, she was tried and convicted of disorderly conduct and of violating local ordinances. A 381-day bus boycott ensued, protesting segregation on public buses.
- Desegregation of Little Rock—in 1957, after the Supreme Court decision on Brown v. Board of Education, which declared "separate but equal" unconstitutional, the Arkansas school board voted to desegregate their schools. Even though Arkansas was considered progressive, its governor brought in the Arkansas National Guard to prevent nine black students from entering Central High School in Little Rock. President Eisenhower responded by federalizing the National Guard and ordering them to stand down.
- Birmingham Campaign—protestors organized a variety of actions such as sit-ins and an organized march to launch a voting campaign. When the City of Birmingham declared the protests illegal, the protestors, including Martin Luther King, Jr., persisted and were arrested and jailed.

Three major pieces of legislation passed as a result of the Civil Rights movement are:

- Brown v. Board of Education (1954)—the Supreme Court declared that "separate but equal" accommodations and services were unconstitutional.
- Civil Rights Act of 1964—this declared discrimination illegal in employment, education, or public accommodation.
- Voting Rights Act of 1965—this act ended various activities practiced, mostly in the South, to bar blacks from exercising their voting rights. These included poll taxes and literacy tests.

Vietnam War

After World War II, the US pledged, as part of its foreign policy, to come to the assistance of any country threatened by communism. When Vietnam was divided into a communist North and democratic South, much like Korea before it, the eventual attempts by the North to unify the country under Communist rule led to intervention by the US. On the home front, the Vietnam War became more and more unpopular politically, with Americans growing increasingly discontent with the inability of the US to achieve the goals it had set for the Asian country. When President Richard Nixon took office in 1969, his escalation of the war led to protests at Kent State in Ohio, during which several students were killed by National Guard troops. Protests continued, eventually resulting in the end of the compulsory draft in 1973. In that same year, the US departed Vietnam. In 1975, the south surrendered, and Vietnam became a unified country under communist rule.

US Cold War foreign policy acts

The following are US Cold War foreign policy acts and how they affected international relationships, especially between the US and the Soviet Union:

- Marshall Plan—this sent aid to war-torn Europe after WWII, largely focusing on preventing the spread of communism.
- Containment Policy—proposed by George F. Kennan, the containment policy focused on containing the spread of Soviet communism.
- Truman Doctrine—Harry S. Truman stated that the US would provide both economic and military support to any country threatened by Soviet takeover.
- National Security Act—passed in 1947, this act reorganized the government's military departments into the Department of Defense, as well as creating the Central Intelligence Agency and the National Security Council.

The combination of these acts led to the Cold War, with Soviet communists attempting to spread their influence and the US and other countries trying to contain or stop this spread.

> ➤ **Review Video:** The Cold War: The United States and Russia
> *Visit* ***mometrix.com/academy*** *and enter* ***Code***: **981433**

NATO, the Warsaw Pact, and the Berlin Wall

NATO, the North Atlantic Treaty Organization, came into being in 1949. It essentially amounted to an agreement among the US and Western European countries that an attack on any one of these countries was to be considered an attack against the entire group.

Under the influence of the Soviet Union, the Eastern European countries of the USSR, Bulgaria, East Germany, Poland, Romania, Albania, Hungary, and Czechoslovakia responded with the Warsaw Pact, which created a similar agreement among those nations.
In 1961, a wall was built to separate communist East Berlin from democratic West Berlin. This was a literal representation of the "Iron Curtain" that separated the democratic and communist countries through the world.

Arms race

After World War II, major nations, particularly the US and USSR, rushed to develop highly advanced weapons systems such as the atomic bomb and later the hydrogen bomb. These countries seemed determined to outpace each other with the development of numerous, deadly weapons. These weapons were expensive and extremely dangerous, and it is possible that the war between US and Soviet interests remained "cold" due to the fear that one side or the other would use these powerful weapons.

End of the Cold War

In the late 1980s, Mikhail Gorbachev led the Soviet Union. He introduced a series of reform programs. Ronald Reagan famously urged Gorbachev to tear down the Berlin Wall as a gesture of growing freedom in the Eastern Bloc, and in 1989 it was demolished, ending the separation of East and West Germany. The Soviet Union relinquished its power over the various republics in Eastern Europe, and they became independent nations with their own individual governments. In 1991, the USSR was dissolved and the Cold War also came to an end.

> ➢ **Review Video:** The Cold War: Resolution
> *Visit **mometrix.com/academy** and enter **Code**: **843092***

Technological advances after WWII

Numerous technological advances after the Second World War led to more effective treatment of diseases, more efficient communication and transportation, and new means of generating power. Advances in medicine increased the human lifespan in developed countries, and near-instantaneous communication opened up a myriad of possibilities. Some of these advances include:

- Discovery of penicillin (1928)
- Supersonic air travel (1947)
- Nuclear power plants (1951)
- Orbital satellite leading to manned space flight (Sputnik, 1957)
- First man on the moon (1969)

US policy toward immigrants after World War II

Prior to WWII, the US had been limiting immigration for several decades. After WWII, policy shifted slightly to accommodate political refugees from Europe and elsewhere. So many people were displaced by the war that in 1946, the UN formed the International Refugee Organization to deal with the problem. In 1948, the US Congress passed the Displaced Persons Act, which allowed over 400,000 European refugees to enter the US, most of them concentration camp survivors and refugees from Eastern Europe.

In 1952, the United States Escapee Program (USEP) increased the quotas, allowing refugees from communist Europe to enter the US, as did the Refugee Relief Act, passed in 1953. At the same time, however, the Internal Security Act of 1950 allowed deportation of declared communists, and Asians were subjected to a quota based on race, rather than country of origin. Later changes included:

- Migration and Refugee Assistance Act (1962)—provided aid for refugees in need
- Immigration and Nationality Act (1965)—ended quotas based on nation of origin
- Immigration Reform and Control Act (1986)—prohibited the hiring of illegal immigrants, but also granted amnesty to about three million illegals already in the country

Expansion of minority rights

Several major acts have been passed, particularly since WWII, to protect the rights of minorities in America. These include:
- Civil Rights Act (1964)
- Voting Rights Act (1965)
- Age Discrimination Act (1967)
- Americans with Disabilities Act (1990)

Other important movements for civil rights included a prisoner's rights movement, movements for immigrant rights, and the women's rights movement. The National Organization for Women (NOW) was established in 1966 and worked to pass the Equal Rights Amendment. The amendment was passed, but not enough states ratified it for it to become part of the US Constitution.

Richard Nixon (R, 1969-1974)

Richard Nixon is best known for the Watergate scandal during his presidency, but other important events marked his tenure as president, including:
- End of the Vietnam War
- Improved diplomatic relations between the US and China, and the US and the USSR
- National Environmental Policy Act passed, providing for environmental protection
- Compulsory draft ended
- Supreme Court legalized abortion in Roe v. Wade
- Watergate

The Watergate scandal of 1972 ended Nixon's presidency. Rather than face impeachment and removal from office, he resigned in 1974.

Gerald Ford (R, 1974-1977)

Gerald Ford was appointed to the vice presidency after Nixon's vice president Spiro Agnew resigned in 1973 under charges of tax evasion. With Nixon's resignation, Ford became president.

Ford's presidency saw negotiations with Russia to limit nuclear arms, as well as struggles to deal with inflation, economic downturn, and energy shortages. Ford's policies sought to reduce governmental control of various businesses and reduce the role of government overall. He also worked to prevent escalation of conflicts in the Middle East.

Jimmy Carter (D, 1977-1981)

Jimmy Carter was elected as president in 1976. Faced with a budget deficit, high unemployment, and continued inflation, Carter also dealt with numerous matters of international diplomacy including:
- Torrijos-Carter Treaties—the US gave control of the Panama Canal to Panama.
- Camp David Accords—negotiations between Anwar el-Sadat, the president of Egypt, and Menachem Begin, the Israeli Prime Minister, led to a peace treaty between Egypt and Israel.

- Strategic Arms Limitation Talks (SALT)—these led to agreements and treaties between the US and the Soviet Union.
- Iran Hostage Crisis—after the Shah of Iran was deposed, an Islamic cleric, Ayatollah Khomeini, came to power. The shah came to the US for medical treatment and Iran demanded his return so he could stand trial. In retaliation, a group of Iranian students stormed the US Embassy in Iran. Fifty-two American hostages were held for 444 days.

Jimmy Carter was awarded the Nobel Peace Prize in 2002.

Ronald Reagan (R, 1981-1989)

Ronald Reagan, at 69, became the oldest American president. The two terms of his administration included notable events such as:
- Reaganomics, also known as supply-side, trickle-down, or free-market economics, involving major tax cuts
- Economic Recovery Tax Act of 1981
- First female justice appointed to the Supreme Court—Sandra Day O'Connor
- Massive increase in the national debt – from $1 trillion to $3 trillion
- Reduction of nuclear weapons via negotiations with Mikhail Gorbachev
- Iran-Contra scandal—cover-up of US involvement in revolutions in El Salvador and Nicaragua
- Deregulation of savings and loan industry
- Loss of the space shuttle *Challenger*

George H. W. Bush (R, 1989-1993)

Reagan's presidency was followed by a term under his former Vice President, George H. W. Bush. Bush's run for president included the famous "thousand points of light" speech, which was instrumental in increasing his standing in the election polls. During Bush's presidency, numerous international events took place, including:
- Fall of the Berlin wall and Germany's unification
- Panamanian dictator Manuel Noriega captured and tried on drug and racketeering charges
- Dissolution of the Soviet Union
- Gulf War, or Operation Desert Storm, triggered by Iraq's invasion of Kuwait
- Tiananmen Square Massacre in Beijing, China
- Ruby Ridge
- The arrival of the World Wide Web

Bill Clinton (D, 1993-2001)

William Jefferson "Bill" Clinton was the second president in US history to be impeached, but he was not convicted, and maintained high approval ratings in spite of the impeachment. Major events during his presidency included:
- Family and Medical Leave Act
- Don't Ask, Don't Tell, a compromise position regarding homosexuals serving in the military
- North American Free Trade Agreement, or NAFTA
- Defense of Marriage Act

- Oslo Accords
- Siege at Waco, Texas, involving the Branch Davidians led by David Koresh
- Bombing of the Murrah Federal Building in Oklahoma City, Oklahoma
- Troops sent to Haiti, Bosnia and Somalia to assist with domestic problems in those areas

George W. Bush (R, 2001-2009)

George W. Bush, son of George Herbert Walker Bush, became president after Clinton. Major events during his presidency included:
- September 11, 2001, al-Qaeda terrorists hijack commercial airliners and fly into the World Trade Center towers and the Pentagon, killing nearly 3000 Americans
- US troops sent to Afghanistan to hunt down al-Qaeda leaders, including the head of the organization, Osama Bin Laden; beginning of the War on Terror
- US troops sent to Iraq, along with a multinational coalition, to depose Saddam Hussein and prevent his deployment of suspected weapons of mass destruction
- Subprime mortgage crisis and near collapse of the financial industry, leading to the Great Recession; first of multiple government bailouts of the financial industry

Barack Obama (D, 2009-2017)

Barack Obama, a first-term senator from Illinois, became the first African-American president. Major events included:
- Multiple bailout packages and spending efforts, in an attempt to inject more money into a stagnant economy
- Massive increase in the national debt – from $10 trillion to $18 trillion
- Reinforcement of the War on Terror in Afghanistan and Iraq; additional deployment of troops in Libya and Syria
- Capture and execution of Osama Bin Laden
- Passage of the Affordable Care Act, legislation that greatly increased government involvement in the healthcare industry, and required every person living in the US to maintain health insurance coverage
- Moves to broaden gay rights, including the repeal of Clinton's Don't Ask, Don't Tell policy for homosexuals serving in the military

Donald Trump (R, 2017-)

Donald Trump, a billionaire real estate tycoon with no prior political experience, was elected to the presidency in a surprise victory over former First Lady and Secretary of State (under Obama) Hillary Clinton. His platform focused on increasing immigration enforcement to curb illegal immigration, restricting foreign trade to improve the dwindling American manufacturing industry, and repealing the Affordable Care Act passed during the prior administration.

Oklahoma History

Mountain ranges

The four major mountain ranges that are located in Oklahoma are the Arbuckle Mountains, the Ouachita Mountains, the Ozark Mountains, and the Wichita Mountains. The Arbuckle Mountains are located in the southern section of Oklahoma, just south of Oklahoma City. These mountains were originally named after Fort Arbuckle, which was a military outpost established in the mountain range in the 1850s by Brigadier General Matthew Arbuckle. The Ouachita Mountains are located in the southeastern section of Oklahoma. These mountains were named after the Ouachita tribe, which originally inhabited the area in which the mountains are located. The Ozark Mountains are located in the northeast section of Oklahoma. The exact origin of the name Ozark is unknown, but the name may originate from the French "aux Arks" or the French "aux arcs." The Wichita Mountains are located in the southwest section of Oklahoma. These mountains were named after the Wichita tribe, which originally inhabited the area that is now Kansas and Oklahoma.

Rivers

The Arkansas River flows from the center of Colorado to the southeastern section of Arkansas. The Arkansas River enters the northeastern side of Oklahoma from Kansas and travels southeast through the cities of Tulsa and Muskogee. The Canadian River, which is also known as the South Canadian River, flows from the southwestern section of Colorado to the eastern section of Oklahoma, where it meets the Arkansas River. The Arkansas River enters the northwestern side of Oklahoma from Texas and travels southeast. The North Canadian River flows from the northeastern section of New Mexico to the center of Oklahoma, where it meets the Canadian River. The North Canadian River enters the northwestern side of Oklahoma from Texas and travels east past Oklahoma City. The Red River flows from the northeastern section of Texas to the center of Louisiana, where it meets the Mississippi River. The Red River enters the southwestern section of Oklahoma from Texas and travels east along the southern border of Oklahoma.

Role in early trade

The rivers of Oklahoma had an important role in the region's early trade because most of the early traders used canoes or other small boats to travel from Canada or Louisiana to the area that is now Oklahoma. The reason for this is that most of the explorers in the area were either French or Spanish, and the Spanish explorers of the time were more interested in treasure than trade. The French, on the other hand, were actually interested in trading with the Native Americans, and the French typically used the rivers to travel to Oklahoma and other nearby areas from their outposts in Canada and Louisiana. As a result, the rivers of Oklahoma were extremely important to the region's early trade because the rivers made it easier for the French traders to transport the goods that they were willing to trade for the animal furs that the Native Americans collected.

Largest cities

The three largest cities in Oklahoma, in terms of population, are Oklahoma City, Tulsa, and Norman. Oklahoma City has the largest population of any city in Oklahoma, with a population of over 550,000. The city is located in the center of Oklahoma on the North Canadian River and is known for its livestock, oil, and natural gas industries. Tulsa has the second largest population of any city in Oklahoma, with a population of over 385,000. The city is located in the northeastern section of Oklahoma on the Arkansas River, and the city is known for the large amount of oil that it has produced since its incorporation in 1898. Norman has the third largest population of any city in Oklahoma, with a population of over 110,000. Norman is located in the center of Oklahoma, just south of the North Canadian River, and the city is known for its colleges and universities, including the University of Oklahoma.

Fort Gibson and Fort Sill

Fort Gibson was originally a military outpost located in the northeast section of Oklahoma that was established to help the U.S. Army protect the area from Native American attack. However, this was not the only purpose that Fort Gibson served, as the fort was also used as an outpost for both the Confederate and the Union forces during the Civil War. The outpost was originally constructed by Colonel Matthew Arbuckle (who was eventually promoted to the rank of brigadier general) on April 20, 1824, but the camp was closed in 1890. Fort Sill is a military outpost located in the southwest section of Oklahoma, just outside the city of Lawton. The fort was originally constructed by Major General Phillip H. Sheridan on January 8, 1869, as a military outpost that the U.S. Army could use to protect the area from Native American attack. The camp is actually still open, but it is now used as an artillery school and a U.S. Marine base.

Five Civilized Tribes

The "Five Civilized Tribes" include the Cherokee, the Chickasaw, the Choctaw, the Muskogee, and the Seminole. The Cherokee and the Muskogee were originally located throughout the area that is now the southeastern United States, but they were forced to leave their lands and march 800 miles to Oklahoma in the late 1830s as the result of the Indian Removal Act. The route that these tribes marched is often known as the Trail of Tears. The Chickasaw and Choctaw were also forced out of the southeastern United States during the 1830s as a result of the Indian Removal Act. However, the Chickasaw specifically inhabited the area that is now Mississippi and Tennessee, and the Choctaw specifically inhabited the area that is now Alabama, Mississippi, and Louisiana before the tribes were forced out. The Seminole were originally located in Florida, and a portion of the tribe was forced to move to Oklahoma. However, a large portion of the tribe actually managed to maintain their lands in Florida in spite of the government's repeated attempts to remove them.

Kiowa Five

The term "Kiowa Five" is typically used to refer to a group of five men from the Kiowa tribe who painted a series of paintings in Oklahoma during the 1920s and 1930s. This group included Spencer Asah, James Auchiah, James Hokeah, Stephen Mopope, and Monroe Tsatoke. However, these five men were not the only members of the "Kiowa Five," and it is important to note that the "Kiowa Five" is sometimes referred to as the "Kiowa Six," because a Kiowa woman by the name of Lois Smoky was also a member of the group for a short period of time in 1927. Each member of the group possessed a number of artistic talents in addition to their painting skills, but they are primarily known for the large number of paintings that they created portraying the ceremonies, stories, and, ultimately, the culture of the Kiowa people.

Quanah Parker

Quanah Parker was a Comanche who originally lived in the area that is now Texas. He fought against the U.S. government as it attempted to force the Comanche off of their ancestral lands, but he was ultimately forced onto a reservation with the rest of the Comanche people in the area that is now the southwestern section of Oklahoma. He was made chief of the Comanche, however, once the tribe arrived at the reservation in 1875, and he fought to protect the Comanche's culture for the rest of his life. In fact, he is well known for establishing a close relationship with a number of powerful white individuals, including Theodore Roosevelt and the wealthy rancher Samuel Burk Burnett. These close relationships allowed Quanah to protect the lands that the Comanche had received on the reservation, to establish a lucrative ranch, and to promote the beliefs that eventually became the foundation for the Native American Church.

Sequoya

Sequoya was a Cherokee who originally lived in the area that is now Alabama. He worked as a silversmith, trading various tools to the white settlers in the area. However, his greatest contribution to the Cherokee people was not a result of his skill as a silversmith, but was instead a result of his skill with the written word. This is because Sequoya actually designed a syllabary, a system of letters and/or symbols in which each represents a specific syllable in the Cherokee language. This syllabary allowed the Cherokee, who up until this time were primarily illiterate, to read and write their own language. Sequoya not only designed the language, however, but he also traveled throughout the Cherokee lands to teach the language to as many people as he could.

Wilma Mankiller

Wilma Mankiller is primarily known for her role as the first woman to serve, and later the first woman to be elected, as the principal chief of the Cherokee Nation. Wilma Mankiller was originally elected to the position of deputy chief of the Cherokee Nation in 1983, and she assumed the position of principal chief when Principal Chief Ross Swimmer resigned in 1985. She was then elected to the position of principal chief in 1987 and again in 1991. During her time as principal chief, Mankiller managed to acquire the funds necessary to carry out a number of projects aimed at increasing the number of tribal businesses and improving the community's resources. Mankiller also helped to strengthen the Cherokee Nation's relations with the federal government, helped to discourage gender bias within the Cherokee Nation, and wrote two books about her life and the history of the Cherokee people.

Louisiana Purchase

The Louisiana Purchase refers to an agreement between the United States and France in which the United States agreed to purchase from France all of the land between the Mississippi River and the area that is now located near the western border of the states of Oklahoma, Colorado, Wyoming, and Montana. This agreement allowed the United States to acquire over 828,000 square miles of land in exchange for $15 million (which was a relatively low price, even at the time.) The Louisiana Purchase agreement, also known as the Louisiana Purchase Treaty, was signed by representatives of President Thomas

Jefferson in Paris on April 30, 1803. The French transferred ownership of New Orleans to the United States on December 20, 1803, before the rest of the land, because acquiring New Orleans was the primary concern of the U.S. However, the remainder of the land, including the land that now makes up most of the state of Oklahoma, was officially transferred to the U.S. on March 10, 1804.

Annexation of Texas and acquisition of the Oklahoma panhandle

The Annexation of Texas refers to an event in U.S. history in which the U.S. Congress passed a joint resolution that allowed Texas to join the United States and become the 28th state in the nation. This gave the U.S. a legitimate claim to some of the land that Mexico controlled because the Republic of Texas had claimed ownership of that land before it had joined the United States. Mexico, however, refused to surrender the land that Texas claimed, and the U.S., at first, attempted to purchase the land from Mexico for $25 million. Mexico refused the offer, and the U.S., as a result, dispatched a small force to claim some of the land that Mexico would not surrender. This action forced the Mexicans to defend the land that they controlled and ultimately caused the Mexican-American War. After the war, the U.S. obtained control of all of the land to which Texas had previously claimed ownership, and a small portion of this land ultimately became the Oklahoma panhandle.

Salina, Oklahoma and the Cherokee Strip

Salina, which is a small town located in northeast Oklahoma, was originally the location of the first permanent trading settlement in Oklahoma. This settlement was established by Jean Pierre Chouteau in 1802 as a location in which the Chouteau family could trade with the Native Americans for the furs that they collected. The demand for fur was extremely high at the time, and the trading post, as a result, was extremely successful. This allowed the Chouteau family to expand the operations at the trading post several times over the next 30 to 40 years, and the trading post continued to bring a large amount of business into the area until the fur trade began to decline in the 1840s. The Cherokee Strip, which is also known as the Cherokee Outlet, refers to an area of land located in northeast Oklahoma that was used to graze cattle. This land originally belonged to the Cherokee, but the federal government took the land after the Civil War and allowed ranchers to use the route to move cattle from Texas to Kansas.

Battle of Honey Springs

The Battle of Honey Springs refers to a battle that took place on the eastern side of Oklahoma near the southeastern edge of Muskogee County. The battle is significant because it was the only major battle fought in Oklahoma during the American Civil War, and it was an important victory for the Union Army. The Battle of Honey Springs began on July 17, 1863, when the Union forces under the command of Major General James G. Blunt attempted to prevent the Confederate forces under the command of Brigadier General Douglas H. Cooper from reaching the Confederate depot at Honey Springs. Cooper's forces were attempting to make their way to the camp because they were dangerously low on men and supplies, and Cooper was hoping that he would be able to resupply his troops and wait for reinforcements. However, Blunt's forces intercepted Cooper's forces before they were able to enter Honey Springs. This allowed Blunt to push the Confederate forces back and seize control of the supply depot at Honey Springs.

Sequoyah Constitutional Convention

The Sequoyah Constitutional Convention played an important role in Oklahoma's movement for statehood. This is because the convention, which took place on August 21, 1905, was the first unified attempt by the Five Civilized Tribes to form a new state. The Five Civilized Tribes (the Cherokee, the Chickasaw, the Choctaw, the Muskogee, and the Seminole) proposed the creation of a Native American state known as the State of Sequoyah that would be separate from the rest of the Oklahoma Territory. However, the federal government denied the convention's petition because it was hoping to have a single state in the area, rather than two distinct states. As a result, William H. Murray, a representative of the Chickasaw Nation, and Charles N. Haskell, a representative of the Muskogee, proposed to hold a second convention to discuss the creation of a state that included the proposed State of Sequoyah and the Oklahoma Territory. This second convention designed a second petition, which ultimately led to the creation of the state of Oklahoma on November 16, 1907.

African Americans

African Americans played an important role in the area that is now Oklahoma both during and after the Civil War. This is partially due to the fact that a large number of African Americans fought in the Union Army. In fact, most of the Union troops at the Battle of Honey Springs were actually African Americans, and it would have been significantly more difficult, if not impossible, for the Union forces to seize Honey Springs if the African American forces under the command of Major James G. Blunt did not aid the white soldiers in intercepting the Confederate forces en route to Honey Springs. However, it is important to note that African Americans also played an important role in developing and protecting the settlements of Oklahoma after the Civil War. In fact, a number of African Americans continued to serve in the U.S. Army after the war to help protect the area from thieves and other threats, while other African Americans went on to compose music, construct cities, open businesses, and perform a variety of other important tasks in Oklahoma.

Hispanics

Hispanic individuals have played an important role in Oklahoma since the state achieved statehood. In fact, much of the Hispanic population that inhabits Oklahoma includes descendants of individuals who immigrated to the United States from Mexico shortly after Oklahoma achieved statehood. These individuals traveled to the United States in the hope that they would be able to find work, food for their families, and a safe place to live because the living conditions in Mexico at the time had begun to decline rapidly. As a result, the Hispanic people quickly became an important part of Oklahoma's labor force, as they began to perform jobs in a number of the state's major industries, including the cotton industry, the mining industry, and the railroad industry.

Asians and Czechs

The Asian population of Oklahoma has always been relatively small. However, many of the Asian individuals living in Oklahoma are descended from individuals who immigrated to the United States from China, Korea, or Japan in 1889 and the years immediately following 1889 to claim some of the land that the U.S. government made available for settlement at that time. Another large portion of the Asian individuals living in Oklahoma are individuals who immigrated from Vietnam after the Vietnam War in the hope of finding work, food, and a safe place to live. The Czech population of Oklahoma has also always been relatively small. However, a large portion of the Czechs living in Oklahoma are descended from individuals who originally immigrated to other parts of the United States from Austria in the mid- to late-1800s and then moved to Oklahoma to claim some of the land that the U.S. government made available for settlement in 1889.

Italians and Germans

The Italian population of Oklahoma was once relatively large, but the number of Italians living in the state has declined since the Great Depression in the 1930s. However, a large portion of the Italians living in Oklahoma are descended from individuals who immigrated to the United States from northern Italy in the late 1800s to find work and claim land. The German population of Oklahoma was also once relatively large, but the number of Germans living in the state declined drastically after the end of World War I. In fact, most of the Germans currently living in Oklahoma immigrated to other parts of the United States from Germany after World War II or are descendants of individuals who immigrated to other parts of the United States from Germany after World War II and moved to Oklahoma to find work.

Temperance movement

The temperance movement refers to a political movement that consisted of a number of individuals who hoped to bring about the complete prohibition of alcoholic beverages in any form. This movement, which originally began in the mid-1600s in the United States, peaked in the 1920s, when the United States passed a federal law outlawing the sale and consumption of alcohol. However, the temperance movement in Oklahoma actually began in the late 1800s, when the Anti-Saloon League (ASL) and other similar temperance groups began advocating the prohibition of alcohol in the Oklahoma Territory. These groups began to hold meetings, pass out anti-alcohol magazines, and gather public support for prohibition, but their ultimate success came when they lobbied for prohibition at the Constitutional Convention for the state of Oklahoma. This is because the temperance groups managed to convince the convention to allow the people of Oklahoma to vote on a constitutional provision that would outlaw the sale and consumption of alcohol. This vote ultimately led to the prohibition of alcohol within the state of Oklahoma, which lasted until 1959.

The Great Depression and the Dust Bowl

The Great Depression refers to a time period in which the economy of the United States and the economy of other nations throughout the world began to decline. This period of economic downturn began when the stock market crashed on October 29, 1929, and the effects of the crash lasted into the early 1940s. This period brought the widespread closure of businesses throughout the world, and, as a result, the unemployment rate skyrocketed throughout Oklahoma and the rest of the nation. It is important to note, however, that the rampant unemployment that occurred in Oklahoma during this time period was actually linked more to the Dust Bowl than the stock market crash. The Dust Bowl refers to a time period in which a drought affected the Great Plains and the surrounding area. This drought, which began in the early 1930s and lasted into the early 1940s, caused the heavily farmed area to dry up and turn to dust. This led to a series of powerful dust storms that inflicted massive damage throughout a number of states, including Oklahoma.

Oil boom

The oil boom in Oklahoma began in the early 1900s, when Frank Chesley and Robert Galbreath discovered oil in the area in which the city of Glenpool is now located. This discovery led to a large influx of individuals who hoped to find oil in the area. These individuals not only brought a large amount of money into the area, as both the wealthy and the poor came in search of oil, but also created new jobs for people both inside and outside the oil industry. This allowed the economy of the area to grow rapidly as the oil industry and the industries that served individuals working in the oil industry continued to expand. Unfortunately, this rapid growth led to a number of problems as individuals attempted to circumvent the laws that existed in the area. In fact, the population of the area quickly became more than the area's law enforcement could handle, and a number of individuals attempted to bribe officials, so they could swindle the Native Americans out of their land rights or conduct other illegal activities.

Ku Klux Klan

The Ku Klux Klan (KKK) is a group that formed shortly after the Civil War to promote white supremacy through a variety of illegal activities that include, but are not limited to, arson, larceny, murder, and voter intimidation. These activities were aimed at discouraging individuals from supporting African American interests and preventing African Americans from participating in society as a whole. The group's activities were focused in the South, but the frequency of these activities began to decline throughout the United States in the 1870s after the government began to crack down on the KKK. There was a resurgence in the KKK, however, in the 1920s, as jobs shifted from the rural communities to the cities, causing a drastic increase in the crime rate. This increase in crime led a number of individuals to support the KKK in the hopes of returning the society of the South to the way it was before the 1920s.

Jim Crow Laws and Sipuel v. Board of Regents of University of Oklahoma

The Jim Crow laws were a series of laws passed in a number of states throughout the late 1800s to the mid-1900s that prohibited African Americans from using the same facilities or, in some cases, the same areas as white Americans. The first Jim Crow law in Oklahoma was passed on December 18, 1907, and it prohibited African Americans from using the same railroad cars, trolley cars, and other forms of public transportation that white Americans used. This law was later followed by a number of other laws that prohibited African Americans from living in the same neighborhoods as white Americans, using the same hospitals as white Americans, and from performing other similar activities. Sipuel v. Board of Regents of University of Oklahoma refers to an Oklahoma court case in which Ada Lois Sipuel filed suit against the University of Oklahoma because the university refused to admit her. The case eventually made its way to the U.S. Supreme Court, which ruled that Sipuel had the right to attend a state school regardless of her skin color.

Tulsa Race Riot

The Tulsa Race Riot refers to an event that took place from May 31, 1921 to June 1, 1921, in which a large group of African Americans attempted to prevent a white mob from lynching an African American man by the name of Dick Rowland. Dick Rowland was a shoe shiner accused of raping a white woman, but there was little evidence to indicate that the accusation was actually true. Unfortunately, this did not stop a lynch mob from making several attempts throughout the evening of May 31, 1921 to take Rowland from the courthouse. The mob's attempts were thwarted by the sheriff each time, but the mob continued its efforts to take Rowland, and word spread to the African American community that the sheriff might need help. This ultimately led to a violent rampage, when a member of the white mob tried to wrestle a gun out of the hands of an African American man offering his aid to the sheriff. This struggle caused the gun that the man was carrying to discharge accidently, and the white mob began to riot.

Government and Political Science

Political science

Political science focuses on studying different governments and how they compare to each other, general political theory, ways political theory is put into action, how nations and governments interact with each other, and a general study of governmental structure and function. Other elements of political science include the study of elections, governmental administration at various levels, development and action of political parties, and how values such as freedom, power, justice and equality are expressed in different political cultures. Political science also encompasses elements of other disciplines, including:

- History—how historical events have shaped political thought and process
- Sociology—the effects of various stages of social development on the growth and development of government and politics
- Anthropology—the effects of governmental process on the culture of an individual group and its relationships with other groups
- Economics—how government policies regulate distribution of products and how they can control and/or influence the economy in general

Government

Based on general political theory, the four major purposes of any given government are:

- Ensuring national security—the government protects against international, domestic and terrorist attacks and also ensures ongoing security through negotiating and establishing relationships with other governments.
- Providing public services—the government should "promote the general welfare," as stated in the Preamble to the US Constitution, by providing whatever is needed to its citizens.
- Ensuring social order—the government supplies means of settling conflicts among citizens as well as making laws to govern the nation, state, or city.
- Making decisions regarding the economy—laws help form the economic policy of the country, regarding both domestic and international trade and related issues. The government also has the ability to distribute goods and wealth to some extent among its citizens.

Origin of the state

There are four main theories regarding the origin of the state:

- Evolutionary—the state evolved from the family, with the head of state the equivalent of the family's patriarch or matriarch.
- Force—one person or group of people brought everyone in an area under their control, forming the first government.
- Divine Right—certain people were chosen by the prevailing deity to be the rulers of the nation, which is itself created by the deity or deities.
- Social Contract—there is no natural order. The people allow themselves to be governed to maintain social order, while the state in turn promises to protect the people they govern. If the government fails to protect its people, the people have the right to seek new leaders.

Influences of philosophers on political study

Ancient Greek philosophers Aristotle and Plato believed political science would lead to order in political matters, and that this scientifically organized order would create stable, just societies.

Thomas Aquinas adapted the ideas of Aristotle to a Christian perspective. His ideas stated that individuals should have certain rights, but also certain duties, and that these rights and duties should determine the type and extent of government rule. In stating that laws should limit the role of government, he laid the groundwork for ideas that would eventually become modern constitutionalism.

Niccolò Machiavelli, author of *The Prince*, was a proponent of politics based on power. He is often considered the founder of modern political science.

Thomas Hobbes, author of *Leviathan* (1651), believed that individual's lives were focused solely on a quest for power, and that the state must work to control this urge. Hobbes felt that people were completely unable to live harmoniously without the intervention of a powerful, undivided government.

John Locke published *Two Treatises of Government* in 1689. This work argued against the ideas of Thomas Hobbes. He put forth the theory of *tabula rasa*—that people are born with minds like blank slates. Individual minds are molded by experience, not innate knowledge or intuition. He also believed that all men should be independent and equal. Many of Locke's ideas found their way into the Constitution of the United States.

The two French philosophers, Montesquieu and Rousseau, heavily influenced the French Revolution (1789-1799). They believed government policies and ideas should change to alleviate existing problems, an idea referred to as "liberalism." Rousseau in particular directly influenced the Revolution with writings such as *The Social Contract* (1762) and *Declaration of the Rights of Man and of the Citizen* (1789). Other ideas Rousseau and Montesquieu espoused included:
- Individual freedom and community welfare are of equal importance
- Man's innate goodness leads to natural harmony
- Reason develops with the rise of civilized society
- Individual citizens carry certain obligations to the existing government

David Hume and Jeremy Bentham believed politics should have as its main goal maintaining "the greatest happiness for the greatest number." Hume also believed in empiricism, or that ideas should not be believed until the proof has been observed. He was a natural skeptic and always sought out the truth of matters rather than believing what he was told.

John Stuart Mill, a British philosopher as well as an economist, believed in progressive policies such as women's suffrage, emancipation, and the development of labor unions and farming cooperatives.

Johann Fichte and Georg Hegel, German philosophers in the late eighteenth and early nineteenth centuries, supported a form of liberalism grounded largely in socialism and a sense of nationalism.

Political orientations

The four main political orientations are:
- Liberal—liberals believe that government should work to increase equality, even at the expense of some freedoms. Government should assist those in need. Focus on enforced social justice and free basic services for everyone.
- Conservative—a conservative believes that government should be limited in most cases. The government should allow its citizens to help one another and solve their own problems rather than enforcing solutions. Business should not be overregulated, allowing a free market.
- Moderate—this ideology incorporates some liberal and some conservative values, generally falling somewhere between in overall belief.
- Libertarian—libertarians believe that the government's role should be limited to protecting the life and liberty of citizens. Government should not be involved in any citizen's life unless that citizen is encroaching upon the rights of another.

Principles of government

The six major principles of government as outlined in the United States Constitution are:
- Federalism—the power of the government does not belong entirely to the national government, but is divided between federal and state governments.
- Popular sovereignty—the government is determined by the people, and gains its authority and power from the people.
- Separation of powers—the government is divided into three branches, executive, legislative, and judicial, with each branch having its own set of powers.
- Judicial review—courts at all levels of government can declare laws invalid if they contradict the constitutions of individual states, or the US Constitution, with the Supreme Court serving as the final judicial authority on decisions of this kind.
- Checks and balances—no single branch can act without input from another, and each branch has the power to "check" any other, as well as balance other branches' powers.
- Limited government—governmental powers are limited and certain individual rights are defined as inviolable by the government.

Powers delegated to the national government

The structure of the US government divides power between national and state governments. Powers delegated to the federal government by the Constitution are:
- Expressed powers—powers directly defined in the Constitution, including power to declare war, regulate commerce, make money, and collect taxes
- Implied powers—powers the national government must have in order to carry out the expressed powers
- Inherent powers—powers inherent to any government, not expressly defined in the Constitution

Some of these powers, such as collection and levying of taxes, are also granted to the individual state governments.

Federalism

The way federalism should be practiced has been the subject of debate since writing of the Constitution. There were—and still are—two main factions regarding this issue:
- States' rights—those favoring the states' rights position feel that the state governments should take the lead in performing local actions to manage various problems.
- Nationalist—those favoring a nationalist position feel the national government should take the lead to deal with those same matters.

The flexibility of the Constitution has allowed the US government to shift and adapt as the needs of the country have changed. Power has often shifted from the state governments to the national government and back again, and both levels of government have developed various ways to influence each other.

Federalism has three major effects on public policy in the US:
- Determining whether the local, state, or national government originates policy
- Affecting how policies are made
- Ensuring policy-making functions under a set of limitations

Federalism also influences the political balance of power in the US by:
- making it difficult, if not impossible, for a single political party to seize total power
- ensuring that individuals can participate in the political system at various levels
- making it possible for individuals working within the system to be able to affect policy at some level, whether local or more widespread

Branches of the US government

The following are the three branches of the US Federal government and the individuals that belong to each branch:
- Legislative Branch—this consists of the two Houses of Congress: the House of Representatives and the Senate. All members of the Legislative Branch are elected officials.
- Executive Branch—this branch is made up of the President, Vice President, presidential advisors, and other various cabinet members. Advisors and cabinet are appointed by the President, but must be approved by Congress.
- Judicial Branch—the federal court system, headed by the Supreme Court.

The three branches of the Federal government each have specific roles and responsibilities:
- The Legislative Branch is largely concerned with law-making. All laws must be approved by Congress before they go into effect. They are also responsible for regulating money and trade, approving presidential appointments, and establishing organizations like the postal service and federal courts. Congress can also propose amendments to the Constitution, and can impeach, or bring charges against, the President. Only Congress can declare war.
- The Executive Branch carries out laws, treaties, and war declarations enacted by Congress. The President can also veto bills approved by Congress, and serves as commander-in-chief of the US military. The president appoints cabinet members, ambassadors to foreign countries, and federal judges.

- The Judicial Branch makes decisions on challenges as to whether laws passed by Congress meet the requirements of the US Constitution. The Supreme Court may also choose to review decisions made by lower courts to determine their constitutionality.

> ➢ **Review Video:** The Three Branches of the US Government
> *Visit **mometrix.com/academy** and enter **Code**: **718704***

US citizenship

Anyone born in the US, born abroad to a US citizen, or who has gone through a process of naturalization is considered a citizen of the United States. It is possible to lose US citizenship as a result of conviction of certain crimes such as treason. Citizenship may also be lost if a citizen pledges an oath to another country or serves in the military of a country engaged in hostilities with the US. A US citizen can also choose to hold dual citizenship, work as an expatriate in another country without losing US citizenship, or even to renounce citizenship if he or she so chooses.

Citizens are granted certain rights under the US government. The most important of these are defined in the Bill of Rights, and include freedom of speech, religion, assembly, and a variety of other rights the government is not allowed to remove. A US citizen also has a number of duties:
- Paying taxes
- Loyalty to the government (though the US does not prosecute those who criticize or seek to change the government)
- Support and defense of the Constitution
- Serving in the Armed Forces when required by law
- Obeying laws as set forth by the various levels of government.

Responsibilities of a US citizen include:
- Voting in elections
- Respecting one another's rights and not infringing on them
- Staying informed about various political and national issues
- Respecting one another's beliefs

Bill of Rights

The first ten amendments of the US Constitution are known as the Bill of Rights. These amendments prevent the government from infringing upon certain freedoms that the founding fathers felt were natural rights that already belonged to all people. These rights included freedom of speech, freedom of religion, the right to bear arms, and freedom of assembly. Many of the rights were formulated in direct response to the way the colonists felt they had been mistreated by the British government.

The first ten amendments were passed by Congress in 1789. Three-fourths of the existing thirteen states had ratified them by December of 1791, making them official additions to the Constitution. The rights granted in the Bill of Rights are:

- First Amendment—freedom of religion, speech, freedom of the press, and the right to assemble and to petition the government
- Second Amendment—the right to bear arms
- Third Amendment—Congress cannot force individuals to house troops
- Fourth Amendment—protection from unreasonable search and seizure
- Fifth Amendment—no individual is required to testify against himself, and no individual may be tried twice for the same crime
- Sixth Amendment—right to criminal trial by jury, right to legal counsel
- Seventh Amendment—right to civil trial by jury
- Eighth Amendment—protection from excessive bail or cruel and unusual punishment
- Ninth Amendment—prevents rights not explicitly named in the Constitution from being taken away because they are not named
- Tenth Amendment—any rights not directly delegated to the national government, or not directly prohibited by the government from the states, belong to the states or to the people

In some cases, the government restricts certain elements of First Amendment rights. Some examples include:

- Freedom of religion—when a religion espouses illegal activities, the government often restricts these forms of religious expression. Examples include polygamy, animal sacrifice, and use of illicit drugs or illegal substances.
- Freedom of speech—this can be restricted if exercise of free speech endangers other people.
- Freedom of the press—laws prevent the press from publishing falsehoods.

In emergency situations such as wartime, stricter restrictions are sometimes placed on these rights, especially rights to free speech and assembly, and freedom of the press, in order to protect national security.

> **Review Video:** The Bill of Rights
> *Visit **mometrix.com/academy** and enter **Code**: 585149*

Constitutional rights of criminals

The US Constitution makes allowances for the rights of criminals, or anyone who has transgressed established laws. There must be laws to protect citizens from criminals, but those accused of crimes must also be protected and their basic rights as individuals preserved. In addition, the Constitution protects individuals from the power of authorities to prevent police forces and other enforcement organizations from becoming oppressive. The fourth, fifth, sixth and eighth amendments specifically address these rights.

Equal protection under the law for all individuals

When the Founding Fathers wrote in the Declaration of Independence that "all men are created equal," they actually were referring to men, and in fact defined citizens as white men who owned land. However, as the country has developed and changed, the definition has expanded to more wholly include all people.

"Equality" does not mean all people are inherently the same, but it does mean they all should be granted the same rights and should be treated the same by the government. Amendments to the Constitution have granted citizenship and voting rights to all Americans regardless of race or gender. The Supreme Court evaluates various laws and court decisions to determine if they properly represent the idea of equal protection. One sample case was Brown v. Board of Education in 1954, which declared separate-but-equal treatment to be unconstitutional.

Civil liberty challenges addressed in current political discussions

The civil rights movements of the 1960s and ongoing struggle for the rights of women and other minorities have sparked challenges to existing law. In addition, debate has raged over how much information the government should be required to divulge to the public. Major issues in today's political climate include:
- Continued debate over women's rights, especially regarding equal pay for equal work
- Debate over affirmative action to encourage hiring of minorities
- Debate over civil rights of homosexuals, including marriage and military service
- Decisions as to whether minorities should be compensated for past discriminatory practices
- Balance between the public's right to know and the government's need to maintain national security
- Balance between the public's right to privacy and national security

Civil liberties and civil rights

While the terms "civil liberties" and "civil rights" are often used synonymously, in actuality their definitions are slightly different. The two concepts work together, however, to define the basics of a free state:
- "Civil liberties" defines the role of the state in providing equal rights and opportunities to individuals within that state. An example is non-discrimination policies with regards to granting citizenship.
- "Civil rights" defines the limitations of governmental rights, describing those rights that belong to individuals and which cannot be infringed upon by the government. Examples of these rights include freedom of religion, political freedom, and overall freedom to live as one chooses.

Suffrage and franchise

Suffrage and franchise both refer to the right to vote. As the US developed as a nation, there was much debate over which individuals should hold this right. In the early years, only white male landowners were granted suffrage. By the nineteenth century, most states had franchised, or granted the right to vote to, all adult white males. The Fifteenth Amendment of 1870 granted suffrage to former slave men. The Nineteenth Amendment gave women the right to vote in 1920, and in 1971 the Twenty-sixth Amendment expanded voting rights to include any US citizen over the age of eighteen. However, those who have not been granted full citizenship and citizens who have committed certain crimes do not have voting rights.

Changes in voting process

The first elections in the US were held by public ballot. However, election abuses soon became common, since public ballot made it easy to intimidate, threaten, or otherwise influence the votes of individuals or groups of individuals. New practices were put into play, including registering voters before elections took place, and using a secret or Australian ballot. In 1892, the introduction of the voting machine further privatized the voting process, since it allowed complete privacy for voting. Today debate continues about the accuracy of various voting methods, including high-tech voting machines and even low-tech punch cards.

Political parties

Different types and numbers of political parties can have a significant effect on how a government is run. If there is a single party, or a one-party system, the government is defined by that one party, and all policy is based on that party's beliefs. In a two-party system, two parties with different viewpoints compete for power and influence. The US is basically a two-party system, with checks and balances to make it difficult for one party to gain complete power over the other. There are also multi-party systems, with three or more parties. In multiparty systems, various parties will often come to agreements in order to form a majority and shift the balance of power.

George Washington was adamantly against the establishment of political parties, based on the abuses perpetrated by such parties in Britain. However, political parties developed in US politics almost from the beginning. Major parties throughout US history have included:
- Federalists and Democratic-Republicans—these parties formed in the late 1700s and disagreed on the balance of power between national and state government.
- Democrats and Whigs—these developed before the Civil War, based on disagreements about various issues such as slavery.
- Democrats and Republicans—the Republican Party developed after the Civil War, and the two parties debated issues centering on the treatment of the post-war South.

While third parties sometimes enter the picture in US politics, the government is basically a two-party system, dominated by the Democrats and Republicans.

> ➤ **Review Video:** Political Parties
> *Visit **mometrix.com/academy** and enter **Code**: 640197*

Functions of political parties

Political parties form organizations at all levels of government. Activities of individual parties include:
- Recruiting and backing candidates for offices
- Discussing various issues with the public, increasing public awareness
- Working toward compromise on difficult issues
- Staffing government offices and providing administrative support

At the administrative level, parties work to ensure that viable candidates are available for elections and that offices and staff are in place to support candidates as they run for office and afterwards, when they are elected.

Process for choosing political candidate

Historically, in the quest for political office, a potential candidate has followed one of the following four processes:

- Nominating convention—an official meeting of the members of a party for the express purpose of nominating candidates for upcoming elections. The Democratic National Convention and the Republican National Convention, convened to announce candidates for presidency, are examples of this kind of gathering.
- Caucus—a meeting, usually attended by a party's leaders. Some states still use caucuses, but not all.
- Primary election—the most common method of choosing candidates today, the primary is a publicly held election to choose candidates.
- Petition—signatures are gathered to place a candidate on the ballot. Petitions can also be used to place legislation on a ballot.

Citizen participation in political process

In addition to voting for elected officials, American citizens are able to participate in the political process through several other avenues. These include:

- Participating in local government
- Participating in caucuses for large elections
- Volunteering to help political parties
- Running for election to local, state, or national offices

Individuals can also donate money to political causes, or support political groups that focus on specific causes such as abortion, wildlife conservation or women's rights. These groups often make use of representatives who lobby legislators to act in support of their efforts.

Campaign funding

Political campaigns are very expensive. In addition to the basic necessities of a campaign office, including office supplies, office space, etc., a large quantity of the money that funds a political campaign goes toward advertising. Money to fund a political campaign can come from several sources including:

- The candidate's personal funds
- Donations by individuals
- Special interest groups

The most significant source of campaign funding is special interest groups. Groups in favor of certain policies will donate money to candidates they believe will support those policies. Special interest groups also do their own advertising in support of candidates they endorse.

Free press and the media

The right to free speech guaranteed in the first amendment to the Constitution allows the media to report on government and political activities without fear of retribution. Because the media has access to information about the government, its policies and actions, as well as debates and discussions that occur in Congress, it can keep the public informed about the inner workings of the government. The media can also draw attention to injustices, imbalances of power, and other transgressions the government or government officials might commit. However, media outlets may, like special interest groups, align themselves with certain political viewpoints and skew their reports to fit that viewpoint. The rise of the Internet has made media reporting even more complex, as news can be found from an infinite variety of sources, both reliable and unreliable.

Anarchism, communism and dictatorship

Anarchists believe that all government should be eliminated and that individuals should rule themselves. Historically, anarchists have used violence and assassination to further their beliefs.

Communism is based on class conflict, revolution and a one-party state. Ideally, a communist government would involve a single government for the entire world. Communist government controls the production and flow of goods and services rather than leaving this to companies or individuals.

Dictatorship involves rule by a single individual. If rule is enforced by a small group, this is referred to as an oligarchy. Dictators tend to rule with a violent hand, using a highly repressive police force to ensure control over the populace.

Fascism and monarchy

Fascism centers on a single leader and is, ideologically, an oppositional belief to communism. Fascism includes a single party state and centralized control. The power of the fascist leader lies in the "cult of personality," and the fascist state often focuses on expansion and conquering of other nations. Monarchy was the major form of government for Europe through most of its history. A monarchy is led by a king or a queen. This position is hereditary, and the rulers are not elected. In modern times, constitutional monarchy has developed, where the king and queen still exist but most of the governmental decisions are made by democratic institutions such as a parliament.

Presidential system and socialism

A presidential system, like a parliamentary system, has a legislature and political parties, but there is no difference between the head of state and the head of government. Instead of separating these functions, an elected president performs both. Election of the president can be direct or indirect, and the president may not necessarily belong to the largest political party. In socialism, the state controls production of goods, though it does not necessarily own all means of production. The state also provides a variety of social services to citizens and helps guide the economy. A democratic form of government often exists in socialist countries.

Totalitarian and authoritarian systems of government

A totalitarian system believes everything should be under the control of the government, from resource production to the press to religion and other social institutions. All aspects of life under a totalitarian system must conform to the ideals of the government. Authoritarian governments practice widespread state authority, but do not necessarily dismantle all public institutions. If a church, for example, exists as an organization but poses no threat to the authority of the state, an authoritarian government might leave it as it is. While all totalitarian governments are by definition authoritarian, a government can be authoritarian without becoming totalitarian.

> **Review Video:** Authoritarian and Totalitarian Systems of Government
> *Visit mometrix.com/academy and enter* **Code: 104046**

Parliamentary and democratic systems of government

In a parliamentary system, government involves a legislature and a variety of political parties. The head of government, usually a Prime Minister, is typically the head of the dominant party. A head of state can be elected, or this position can be taken by a monarch, as in Great Britain's constitutional monarchy system.

In a democratic system of government, the people elect their government representatives. The word "democracy" is a Greek term that means "rule of the people." There are two forms of democracy—direct and indirect. In a direct democracy, each issue or election is decided by a vote where each individual is counted separately. An indirect democracy employs a legislature that votes on issues that affect large numbers of people whom the legislative members represent. Democracy can exist as a parliamentary system or a presidential system. The US is a presidential, indirect democracy.

Realism, liberalism, institutionalism, and constructivism

The theory of realism states that nations are by nature aggressive, and work in their own self-interest. Relations between nations are determined by military and economic strength. The nation is seen as the highest authority. Liberalism believes states can cooperate, and that they act based on capability rather than power. This term was originally coined to describe Woodrow Wilson's theories on international cooperation. In institutionalism, institutions provide structure and incentive for cooperation among nations. Institutions are defined as a set of rules used to make international decisions. These institutions also help distribute power and determine how nations will interact. Constructivism, like liberalism, is based on international cooperation, but recognizes that perceptions countries have of each other can affect their relations.

> **Review Video:** Classical Liberalism
> *Visit mometrix.com/academy and enter* **Code: 535938**

Foreign policy

Foreign policy is a set of goals, policies and strategies that determine how an individual nation will interact with other countries. These strategies shift, sometimes quickly and drastically, according to actions or changes occurring in the other countries. However, a nation's foreign policy is often based on a certain set of ideals and national needs.

Examples of US foreign policy include isolationism versus internationalism. In the 1800s, the US leaned more toward isolationism, exhibiting a reluctance to become involved in foreign affairs. The World Wars led to a period of internationalism, as the US entered these wars in support of other countries and joined the United Nations. Today's foreign policy tends more toward interdependence, or globalism, recognizing the widespread affects of issues like economic health. US foreign policy is largely determined by Congress and the president, influenced by the secretary of state, secretary of defense, and the national security adviser. Executive officials carry out policies. The main departments in charge of these day-to-day issues are the US Department of State, also referred to as the State Department. The Department of State carries out policy, negotiates treaties, maintains diplomatic relations, assists citizens traveling in foreign countries, and ensures that the president is properly informed of any international issues. The Department of Defense, the largest executive department in the US, supervises the armed forces and provides assistance to the President in his role as Commander-in-chief.

International organizations

Two types of international organizations are:
- Intergovernmental organizations (IGOs). These organizations are made up of members from various national governments. The UN is an example of an intergovernmental organization. Treaties among the member nations determine the functions and powers of these groups.
- Nongovernmental organizations (NGOs). An NGO lies outside the scope of any government and is usually supported through private donations. An example of an NGO is the International Red Cross, which works with governments all over the world when their countries are in crisis, but is formally affiliated with no particular country or government.

Diplomats

Diplomats are individuals who reside in foreign countries in order to maintain communications between that country and their home country. They help negotiate trade agreements and environmental policies, as well as conveying official information to foreign governments. They also help to resolve conflicts between the countries, often working to sort out issues without making the conflicts official in any way. Diplomats, or ambassadors, are appointed in the US by the president. Appointments must be approved by Congress.

UN

The United Nations (UN) helps form international policies by hosting representatives of various countries who then provide input into policy decisions. Countries who are members of the UN must agree to abide by all final UN resolutions, but this is not always the case in practice, as dissent is not uncommon. If countries do not follow UN resolutions, the UN can decide on sanctions against those countries, often economic sanctions, such as trade restriction. The UN can also send military forces to problem areas, with "peace keeping" troops brought in from member nations. An example of this function is the Korean War, the first war in which an international organization played a major role.

Economics

Economics

Economics is the study of the ways specific societies allocate resources to individuals and groups within that society. Also important are the choices society makes regarding what efforts or initiatives are funded and which are not. Since resources in any society are finite, allocation becomes a vivid reflection of that society's values. In general, the economic system that drives an individual society is based on:
- What goods are produced
- How those goods are produced
- Who acquires the goods or benefits from them

Economics consists of two main categories: macroeconomics, which studies larger systems, and microeconomics, which studies smaller systems.

Market economy

A market economy is based on supply and demand. Demand has to do with what customers want and need, as well as what quantity those consumers are able to purchase based on other economic factors. Supply refers to how much can be produced to meet demand, or how much suppliers are willing and able to sell. Where the needs of consumers meet the needs of suppliers is referred to as a market equilibrium price. This price varies depending on many factors, including the overall health of a society's economy, overall beliefs and considerations of individuals in society. The following is a list of terms defined in the context of a market economy:
- Elasticity—this is based on how the quantity of a particular product responds to the price demanded for that product. If quantity responds quickly to changes in price, the supply/demand for that product is said to be elastic. If it does not respond quickly, then the supply/demand is inelastic.
- Market efficiency—this occurs when a market is capable of producing output high enough to meet consumer demand, that market is efficient.
- Comparative advantage—in the field of international trade, this refers to a country focusing on a specific product that it can produce it more efficiently and more cheaply, or at a lower opportunity cost, than another country, thus giving it a comparative advantage in production.

> ➢ **Review Video:** Market Economy
> *Visit **mometrix.com/academy** and enter **Code: 460547***

Comparison to planned economy

In a market economy, supply and demand are determined by consumers. In a planned economy, a public entity or planning authority makes the decisions about what resources will be produced, how they will be produced, and who will be able to benefit from them. The means of production, such as factories, are also owned by a public entity rather than by private interests. In market socialism, the economic structure falls somewhere between the market economy and the planned economy. Planning authorities determine allocation of resources at higher economic levels, while consumer goods are driven by a market economy.

Microeconomics

While economics generally studies how resources are allocated, microeconomics focuses on economic factors such as the way consumers behave, how income is distributed, and output and input markets. Studies are limited to the industry or firm level, rather than an entire country or society. Among the elements studied in microeconomics are factors of production, costs of production, and factor income. These factors determine production decisions of individual firms, based on resources and costs.

> ➤ **Review Video:** Microeconomics
> *Visit mometrix.com/academy and enter* **Code: 779207**

Classification of markets

The conditions prevailing in a given market are used to classify markets. Conditions considered include:
- Existence of competition
- Number and size of suppliers
- Influence of suppliers over price
- Variety of available products
- Ease of entering the market

Once these questions are answered, an economist can classify a certain market according to its structure and the nature of competition within the market.

Market failure

When any of the elements for a successfully competitive market are missing, this can lead to a market failure. Certain elements are necessary to create what economists call "perfect competition." If one of these factors is weak or lacking, the market is classified as having "imperfect competition." Worse than imperfect competition, though, is a market failure. There are five major types of market failure:
- Inadequate competition
- Inadequate information
- Immobile resources
- Negative externalities, or side effects
- Failure to provide public goods

Externalities are side effects of a market that affect third parties. These effects can be either negative or positive.

> ➤ **Review Video:** Market Failure
> *Visit mometrix.com/academy and enter* **Code: 198450**

Factors of production and costs of production

Every good and service requires certain resources, or inputs. These inputs are referred to as factors of production. Every good and service requires four factors of production:
- Labor
- Capital
- Land
- Entrepreneurship

These factors can be fixed or variable, and can produce fixed or variable costs. Examples of fixed costs include land and equipment. Variable costs include labor. The total of fixed and variable costs makes up the cost of production.

Factor income

Factors of production each have an associated factor income. Factors that earn income include:
- Labor—earns wages
- Capital—earns interest
- Land—earns rent
- Entrepreneurship—earns profit

Each factor's income is determined by its contribution. In a market economy, this income is not guaranteed to be equal. How scarce the factor is and the weight of its contribution to the overall production process determines the final factor income.

Output market

The four kinds of market structures in an output market are:
- Perfect competition—all existing firms sell an identical product. The firms are not able to control the final price. In addition, there is nothing that makes it difficult to become involved in or leave the industry. Anything that would prevent entering or leaving an industry is called a barrier to entry. An example of this market structure is agriculture.
- Monopoly—a single seller controls the product and its price. Barriers to entry, such as prohibitively high fixed cost structures, prevent other sellers from entering the market.
- Monopolistic competition—a number of firms sell similar products, but they are not identical, such as different brands of clothes or food. Barriers to entry are low.
- Oligopoly—only a few firms control the production and distribution of products, such as automobiles. Barriers to entry are high, preventing large numbers of firms from entering the market.

Monopolies

Four types of monopolies are:
- Natural monopoly—a single supplier has a distinct advantage over the others.
- Geographic monopoly—only one business offers the product in a certain area.
- Technological monopoly—a single company controls the technology necessary to supply the product.
- Government monopoly—a government agency is the only provider of a specific good or service.

Control by the US government
The US government has passed several acts to regulate businesses, including:
- Sherman Antitrust Act (1890)—this prohibited trusts, monopolies, and any other situations that eliminated competition.
- Clayton Antitrust Act (1914)—this prohibited price discrimination.
- Robinson-Patman Act (1936)—this strengthened provisions of the Clayton Antitrust Act, requiring businesses to offer the same pricing on products to any customer.

The government has also taken other actions to ensure competition, including requirements for public disclosure. The Securities and Exchange Commission (SEC) requires companies that provide public stock to provide financial reports on a regular basis. Because of the nature of their business, banks are further regulated and required to provide various information to the government.

Marketing and utility

Marketing consists of all of the activity necessary to convince consumers to acquire goods. One major way to move products into the hands of consumers is to convince them that any single product will satisfy a need. The ability of a product or service to satisfy the need of a consumer is called utility. There are four types of utility:
- Form utility—a product's desirability lies in its physical characteristics.
- Place utility—a product's desirability is connected to its location and convenience.
- Time utility—a product's desirability is determined by its availability at a certain time.
- Ownership utility—a product's desirability is increased because ownership of the product passes to the consumer.

Marketing behavior will stress any or all of these types of utility when marketing to the consumer.

Determining a product's market

Successful marketing depends not only on convincing customers they need the product, but also on focusing the marketing towards those who already have a need or desire for the product. Before releasing a product into the general marketplace, many producers will test markets to determine which will be the most receptive to the product.

There are three steps usually taken to evaluate a product's market:
- Market research—this involves researching a market to determine if it will be receptive to the product.
- Market surveys—a part of market research, market surveys ask consumers specific questions to help determine the marketability of a product to a specific group.
- Test marketing—this includes releasing the product into a small geographical area to see how it sells. Often test marketing is followed by wider marketing if the product does well.

Marketing plan

Once these elements have all been determined, the producer can proceed with production and distribution of his product.
- Product—this includes any elements pertaining directly to the product, such as packaging, presentation, or services to include along with it.
- Price—this calculates cost of production, distribution, advertising, etc., as well as the desired profit to determine the final price.
- Place—this determines which outlets will be used to sell the product, whether traditional outlets or through direct mail or Internet marketing.
- Promotion—this involves ways to let consumers know the product is available, through advertising and other means.

> ➤ **Review Video:** Marketing Plan
> *Visit **mometrix.com/academy** and enter **Code**: 983409*

Distribution channels

Distribution channels determine the route a product takes on its journey from producer to consumer, and can also influence the final price and availability of the product. There are two major forms of distributions: wholesale and retail. A wholesale distributor buys in large quantities and then resells smaller amounts to other businesses. Retailers sell directly to the consumers rather than to businesses. In the modern marketplace, additional distribution channels have grown up with the rise of markets such as club warehouse stores as well as purchasing through catalogs or over the Internet. Most of these newer distribution channels bring products more directly to the consumer, eliminating the need for middlemen.

Distribution of income and poverty

Distribution of income in any society ranges from poorest to richest. In most societies, income is not distributed evenly. To determine income distribution, family incomes are ranked from lowest to highest. These rankings are divided into five sections called quintiles, which are compared to each other. The uneven distribution of income is often linked to higher levels of education and ability in the upper classes, but can also be due to other factors such as discrimination and existing monopolies. The income gap in America continues to grow, largely due to growth in the service industry, changes in the American family unit and reduced influence of labor unions. Poverty is defined by comparing incomes to poverty guidelines. Poverty guidelines determine the level of income necessary for a family to function. Those below the poverty line are often eligible for assistance from government agencies.

Consumer behavior

The two major types of consumer behavior as defined in macroeconomics are:
- Marginal propensity to consume defines the tendency of consumers to increase spending in conjunction with increases in income. In general, individuals with greater income will buy more. As individuals increase their income through job changes or growth of experience, they will also increase spending.
- Utility is a term that describes the satisfaction experienced by a consumer in relation to acquiring and using a good or service. Providers of goods and services will stress utility to convince consumers they want the products being presented.

Macroeconomics

Macroeconomics examines economies on a much larger level than microeconomics. While microeconomics studies economics on a firm or industry level, macroeconomics looks at economic trends and structures on a national level. Variables studied in macroeconomics include:
- Output
- Consumption
- Investment
- Government spending
- Net exports

The overall economic condition of a nation is defined as the Gross Domestic Product, or GDP. GDP measures a nation's economic output over a limited time period, such as a year.

> **Review Video:** Microeconomics and Macroeconomics
> *Visit **mometrix.com/academy** and enter **Code**: 538837*

GDP

The two major ways to measure the Gross Domestic Product of a country are:
- The expenditures approach calculates the GDP based on how much money is spent in each individual sector.
- The income approach calculates the GDP based on how much money is earned in each sector.

Both methods yield the same results and both of these calculation methods are based on four economic sectors that make up a country's macro-economy:
- Consumers
- Business
- Government
- Foreign sector

Several factors must be considered in order to accurately calculate the GDP using the incomes approach. Income factors are:
- Wages paid to laborers, or Compensation of Employees
- Rental income derived from land
- Interest income derived from invested capital
- Entrepreneurial income

Entrepreneurial income consists of two forms. Proprietor's income is income that comes back to the entrepreneur himself. Corporate profit is income that goes back into the corporation as a whole. Corporate profit is divided by the corporation into corporate profits taxes, dividends, and retained earnings. Two other figures must be subtracted in the incomes approach. These are indirect business taxes, including property and sales taxes, and depreciation.

Effects of the population
Changes in population can affect the calculation of a nation's GDP, particularly since GDP and GNP (Gross National Product) are generally measured per capita. If a country's economic production is low, but the population is high, the income per individual will be lower than if the income is high and the population is lower. Also, if the population grows quickly and the income grows slowly, individual income will remain low or even drop drastically. Population growth can also affect overall economic growth. Economic growth requires both that consumers purchase goods and workers produce them. A population that does not grow quickly enough will not supply enough workers to support rapid economic growth.

Ideal balance in an economy and phases in national economies
Ideally, an economy functions efficiently, with the aggregate supply, or the amount of national output, equal to the aggregate demand, or the amount of the output that is purchased. In these cases, the economy is stable and prosperous. However, economies more typically go through phases. These phases are:
- Boom—GDP is high and the economy prospers
- Recession—GDP falls, unemployment rises
- Trough—the recession reaches its lowest point
- Recovery—unemployment lessens, prices rise, and the economy begins to stabilize again

These phases tend to repeat in cycles that are not necessarily predictable or regular.

Unemployment and inflation

When demand outstrips supply, prices are driven artificially high, or inflated. This occurs when too much spending causes an imbalance in the economy. In general, inflation occurs because an economy is growing too quickly. When there is too little spending and supply has moved far beyond demand, a surplus of product results. Companies cut back on production, reduce the number of employees, and unemployment rises as people lose their jobs. This imbalance occurs when an economy becomes sluggish. In general, both these economic instability situations are caused by an imbalance between supply and demand. Government intervention may be necessary to stabilize an economy when either inflation or unemployment becomes too serious.

<u>Forms of unemployment</u>
- Frictional—when workers change jobs and are unemployed while waiting for new jobs
- Structural—when economic shifts reduce the need for workers
- Cyclical—when natural business cycles bring about loss of jobs
- Seasonal—when seasonal cycles reduce the need for certain jobs
- Technological—when advances in technology result in elimination of certain jobs

Any of these factors can increase unemployment in certain sectors. Inflation is classified by the overall rate at which it occurs:
- Creeping inflation—this is an inflation rate of about 1-3% annually.
- Walking inflation—this is an inflation rate of 3-10% annually.
- Galloping inflation—this is a high inflation rate of more than 10% but less than 1000% annually.
- Hyperinflation—this is an inflation rate over 1000% per year. Hyperinflation usually leads to complete monetary collapse in a society, as individuals become unable to generate sufficient income to purchase necessary goods.

<u>Government intervention policies</u>
When an economy becomes too imbalanced, either due to excessive spending or not enough spending, government intervention often becomes necessary to put the economy back on track. Government Fiscal Policy can take several forms, including:
- Contractionary policy
- Expansionary policy
- Monetary policy

Contractionary policies help counteract inflation. These include increasing taxes and decreasing government spending to slow spending in the overall economy. Expansionary policies increase government spending and lower taxes in order to reduce unemployment and increase the level of spending in the economy overall. Monetary policy can take several forms, and affects the amount of funds available to banks for making loans.

Populations and population growth

Populations are studied by size, rates of growth due to immigration, the overall fertility rate, and life expectancy. For example, though the population of the United States is considerably larger than it was two hundred years ago, the rate of population growth has decreased greatly, from about three percent per year to less than one percent per year. In the US, the fertility rate is fairly low, with most choosing not to have large families, and life expectancy is high, creating a projected imbalance between older and younger people in the near future. In addition, immigration and the mixing of racially diverse cultures are projected to increase the percentages of Asians, Hispanics and African-Americans.

Money

Money is used in three major ways:
- As an accounting unit
- As a store of value
- As an exchange medium

In general, money must be acceptable throughout a society in exchange for debts or to purchase goods and services. Money should be relatively scarce, its value should remain stable, and it should be easily carried, durable, and easy to divide up. There are three basic types of money: commodity, representative and fiat. Commodity money includes gems or precious metals. Representative money can be exchanged for items such as gold or silver which have inherent value. Fiat money, or legal tender, has no inherent value but has been declared to function as money by the government. It is often backed by gold or silver, but not necessarily on a one-to-one ratio.

<u>US money</u>
Money in the US is not just currency. When economists calculate the amount of money available, they must take into account other factors such as deposits that have been placed in checking accounts, debit cards and "near moneys" such as savings accounts, that can be quickly converted into cash. Currency, checkable deposits and traveler's checks, referred to as M1, are added up, and then M2 is calculated by adding savings deposits, CDs and various other monetary deposits. The final result is the total quantity of available money.

Monetary policy and the Federal Reserve System

The Federal Reserve System, also known as the Fed, implements all monetary policy in the US. Monetary policy regulates the amount of money available in the American banking system. The Fed can decrease or increase the amount of available money for loans, thus helping regulate the national economy. Monetary policies implemented by the Fed are part of expansionary or contractionary monetary policies that help counteract inflation or unemployment. The discount rate is an interest rate charged by the Fed when banks borrow money from them. A lower discount rate leads banks to borrow more money, leading to increased spending. A higher discount rate has the opposite effect.

> **Review Video:** <u>Monetary Policy</u>
> *Visit **mometrix.com/academy** and enter **Code**: 662298*

Banks

Banks earn their income by loaning out money and charging interest on those loans. If less money is available, fewer loans can be made, which affects the amount of spending in the overall economy. While banks function by making loans, they are not allowed to loan out all the money they hold in deposit. The amount of money they must maintain in reserve is known as the reserve ratio. If the reserve ratio is raised, less money is available for loans and spending decreases. A lower reserve ratio increases available funds and increases spending. This ratio is determined by the Federal Reserve System.

Open Market Operations

The Federal Reserve System can also expand or contract the overall money supply through open market operations. In this case, the Fed can buy or sell bonds it has purchased from banks or individuals. When the Fed buys bonds, more money is put into circulation, creating an expansionary situation to stimulate the economy. When the Fed sells bonds, money is withdrawn from the system, creating a contractionary situation to slow an economy suffering from inflation. Because of international financial markets, however, American banks often borrow and lend money in markets outside the US. By shifting their attention to international markets, domestic banks and other businesses can circumvent whatever contractionary policies the Fed may have put into place.

International trade

International trade can take advantage of broader markets, bringing a wider variety of products within easy reach. By contrast, it can also allow individual countries to specialize in particular products that they can produce easily, such as those for which they have easy access to raw materials. Other products, more difficult to make domestically, can be acquired through trade with other nations. International trade requires efficient use of native resources as well as sufficient disposable income to purchase native and imported products. Many countries in the world engage extensively in international trade, but others still face major economic challenges.

Developing nations

The five major characteristics of a developing nation are:
- Low GDP
- Rapid growth of population
- Economy that depends on subsistence agriculture
- Poor conditions, including high infant mortality rates, high disease rates, poor sanitation, and insufficient housing
- Low literacy rate

Developing nations often function under oppressive governments that do not provide private property rights and withhold education and other rights from women. They also often feature an extreme disparity between upper and lower classes, with little opportunity for the lower classes to improve their position.

Stages of economic development
Economic development occurs in three stages that are defined by the activities that drive the economy:
- Agricultural stage
- Manufacturing stage
- Service sector stage

In developing countries, it is often difficult to acquire the necessary funding to provide equipment and training to move into the advanced stages of economic development. Some can receive help from developed countries via foreign aid and investment or international organizations such as the International Monetary Fund or the World Bank. Having developed countries provide monetary, technical, or military assistance can help developing countries move forward to the next stage in their development.

Obstacles to economic growth
Developing nations typically struggle to overcome obstacles that prevent or slow economic development. Major obstacles can include:
- Rapid, uncontrolled population growth
- Trade restrictions
- Misused resources, often perpetrated by the government
- Traditional beliefs that can slow or reject change

Corrupt, oppressive governments often hamper the economic growth of developing nations, creating huge economic disparities and making it impossible for individuals to advance, in turn preventing overall growth. Governments sometimes export currency, called capital flight, which is detrimental to a country's economic development. In general, countries are more likely to experience economic growth if their governments encourage entrepreneurship and provide private property rights.

Problems with rapid industrialization

Rapid growth throughout the world leaves some nations behind, and sometimes spurs their governments to move forward too quickly into industrialization and artificially rapid economic growth. While slow or nonexistent economic growth causes problems in a country, overly rapid industrialization carries its own issues. Four major problems encountered due to rapid industrialization are:

- Use of technology not suited to the products or services being supplied
- Poor investment of capital
- Lack of time for the population to adapt to new paradigms
- Lack of time to experience all stages of development and adjust to each stage

Economic failures in Indonesia were largely due to rapid growth that was poorly handled.

E-commerce

The growth of the Internet has brought many changes to our society, not the least of which is the modern way of business. Where supply channels used to move in certain necessary ways, many of these channels are now bypassed as e-commerce makes it possible for nearly any individual to set up a direct market to consumers, as well as direct interaction with suppliers. Competition is fierce. In many instances e-commerce can provide nearly instantaneous gratification, with a wide variety of products. Whoever provides the best product most quickly often rises to the top of a marketplace. How this added element to the marketplace will affect the economy in the future remains to be seen. Many industries are still struggling with the best ways to adapt to the rapid, continuous changes.

Knowledge economy

The knowledge economy is a growing sector in the economy of developed countries, and includes the trade and development of:

- Data
- Intellectual property
- Technology, especially in the area of communications

Knowledge as a resource is steadily becoming more and more important. What is now being called the Information Age may prove to bring about changes in life and culture as significant as those brought on by the Agricultural and Industrial Revolutions.

Cybernomics

Related to the knowledge economy is what has been dubbed "cybernomics," or economics driven by e-commerce and other computer-based markets and products. Marketing has changed drastically with the growth of cyber communication, allowing suppliers to connect one-on-one with their customers. Other issues coming to the fore regarding cybernomics include:

- Secure online trade
- Intellectual property rights
- Rights to privacy
- Bringing developing nations into the fold

As these issues are debated and new laws and policies developed, the face of many industries continues to undergo drastic change. Many of the old ways of doing business no longer work, leaving industries scrambling to function profitably within the new system.

Practice Test

Practice Questions

1. Which of the following rivers is NOT a major Oklahoma river?
   a. The Red River
   b. The Pecos River
   c. The Canadian River
   d. The Arkansas River

2. Of the following Oklahoma lakes, which two are closest to Oklahoma City?
   a. Lake Eufaula and Sardis Lake
   b. Lake Texoma and Atoka Lake
   c. Arcadia Lake and Lake Thunderbird
   d. Tom Steed Lake and Lake Altus-Lugert

3. Which of the following is true about the relationship of Oklahoma's natural resources to its economic development from 1900 to 1930?
   a. Employment more than tripled during this period.
   b. The state's population quadrupled during this period.
   c. Agriculture, the state's main activity, grew even more.
   d. Dominant industries included oil and meat but not cotton.

4. Which of the following is true about the Native American Sequoyah?
   a. He was born in Oklahoma.
   b. He lived his whole life in Oklahoma.
   c. He fought in the War of 1812 for the Creek Indians.
   d. He invented the first written Cherokee language alphabet.

5. Of the following, which is MOST accurate regarding Quanah Parker?
   a. He rejected the "white man's road."
   b. He embraced the "white man's road."
   c. He preserved his Comanche heritage.
   d. He did both (B) and (C) rather than (A).

6. Who is/are the artist(s) from the Kiowa Five who later painted murals on the Anadarko Post Office under FDR's 1930s Works Progress Administration (WPA), which are still there today?
   a. Jack Hokeah
   b. Monroe Tsatoke
   c. Stephen Mopope
   d. Spencer Asah and James Auchiah

7. Which of the following is true about Wilma Mankiller?
    a. She was the first woman elected principal chief of the Cherokee Nation and was reelected twice.
    b. She was a women's rights activist and improved Cherokee health care, education, and government.
    c. She published two books, one with a foreword by Gloria Steinem, and taught at Dartmouth College.
    d. She achieved all these, the Presidential Medal of Freedom, and President Obama's posthumous tribute.

8. In the history of territorial acquisitions related to Oklahoma, which occurred first?
    a. The Oklahoma Panhandle was ceded to the Spanish government in return for Florida Territory.
    b. The land that is the state of Oklahoma today was acquired by the United States in the Louisiana Purchase.
    c. The U.S. government's Indian Removal Act forced Seminole tribes to relocate to Indian Territory.
    d. The Oklahoma Territory was formally designated by U.S. Congress via the Oklahoma Organic Act.

9. Which statement is most accurate about Oklahoma's Indian Territory during the Civil War?
    a. The Confederate forces controlled it throughout the war.
    b. The Union forces maintained control throughout the war.
    c. Early Confederate–tribal alliances defeated Union forces.
    d. The last surrendering Confederate general was Cherokee.

10. Oklahoma became America's __ state in ____.
    a. 40th; 1900
    b. 43rd; 1902
    c. 45th; 1905
    d. 46th; 1907

11. Among the following events in Oklahoma cattle industry history, which one occurred the latest?
    a. The Civil War caused the Five Civilized Nations to lose more than 300,000 cattle.
    b. The Cherokee Outlet Opening for settlement terminated open-range grazing.
    c. The California Gold Rush created a market for huge herds of open-range cattle.
    d. Texas cattle drives created an economic boom on the Chisholm and Western Trails.

12. During the settlement of Oklahoma, which of these is accurate regarding European immigrants?
    a. In the year 1910, more than 2 percent of Oklahoma's population consisted of immigrants.
    b. Large German and Russian populations lived in Pittsburg County in the 1900s.
    c. Polish and Italian miners inhabited the Washita River area early in the 1900s.
    d. A large Czech ethnic community settled in Enid in north central Oklahoma.

13. Which of the following is true about Oklahoma during the Great Depression?
    a. Oklahoma agriculture had been booming for the 10 years before the Depression.
    b. The regional drought in 1930 exacerbated the decade-long agricultural difficulties.
    c. Oil production in east Texas did not compete with Oklahoma until the later 1930s.
    d. The economy of Oklahoma declined until it reached an all-time low from 1935 to 1936.

14. Regarding prohibition laws in response to the temperance movement, which of these is true about Oklahoma?
    a. Oklahoma originally included prohibition in its state constitution when it became U.S. state.
    b. Oklahoma's first prohibition was in compliance with U.S. prohibition law during World War I.
    c. Oklahoma was included in the first group of states that voted to ratify the 18th Amendment.
    d. Oklahoma was included in the states that ratified the 18th Amendment after it was passed.

15. Regarding the multiple factors contributing to the Dust Bowl in 1930s Oklahoma, which of these MOST accurately represents the sequence in which they occurred?
    a. Overgrazing; farming methods; drought; erosion
    b. Erosion; drought; farming methods; overgrazing
    c. Drought; overgrazing; erosion; farming methods
    d. Farming methods; erosion; overgrazing; drought

16. Which of the following is correct regarding the oil boom and bust in Oklahoma history?
    a. There was a single oil boom in Tulsa, Oklahoma, from 1901 to 1907.
    b. There were two oil booms in Tulsa, Oklahoma: from 1901 to 1907 and 1915 to 1930.
    c. The oil bust happened in Tulsa, Oklahoma, between 1940 and 1960.
    d. The oil bust in Tulsa, Oklahoma, took place between 1960 and 1980.

17. In which areas were Jim Crow laws most commonly passed in Oklahoma from 1954 to 1957?
    a. All of these areas.
    b. Voting rights, education, and railroads
    c. Entertainment, public carriers, and health care
    d. Public accommodations, miscegenation, and adoption

18. Among the background factors contributing to the Tulsa Race Riot, which of these came first?
    a. A Tulsa city ordinance mandated residential segregation, ignoring the Supreme Court.
    b. White immigrants competing with blacks for jobs led race riots during Red Summer.
    c. The presence of the Ku Klux Klan became prominent in Oklahoma, specifically in Tulsa.
    d. A potential lynch mob's formation over unsubstantiated assault rumors led to gunfire.

19. Among landmark Supreme Court civil rights cases from Oklahoma, which of these occurred the most recently?
 a. In *Guinn v. United States*, the Supreme Court struck down a grandfather clause exempting white voters from a required literacy test.
 b. In *Lane v. Wilson*, the Supreme Court struck down a state law that racially manipulated voting by putting a time limit on registration.
 c. In *Sipuel v. Board of Regents of University of Oklahoma*, the Supreme Court required Oklahoma to admit a black woman into law school.
 d. In *McLaurin v. Oklahoma State Regents*, the Supreme Court set the precedent with higher education for *Brown v. Board of Education*.

20. Which of these is true about former Oklahoma Governor Raymond Gary?
 a. He ordered the Oklahoma State Capitol restrooms be desegregated.
 b. He supported and enforced the *Brown v. Board of Education* ruling.
 c. He was not involved in Oklahoma politics before becoming governor.
 d. He accomplished both (A) and also (B), but (C) is not true about him.

21. What grassroots political movement, started by southern and western farmers, arose in the 1890s U.S. to fight banks, railroads, large corporations and other "elites"?
 a. Entrepreneurship Movement
 b. Farmers United
 c. Populist Movement
 d. Social Gospel Movement

22. Which characteristic has NOT yet been used to define a historical era in U.S. History?
 a. A land form
 b. Years of war
 c. Years of social reforms
 d. A time of economic growth or failure

23. Which turning point event in the Spanish-American War occurred in 1898?
 a. America gave financial support to Cuban nationalists' revolution against Spain.
 b. Americans blamed Spain for the sinking of the *USS Maine*.
 c. The Philippines declared independence from U.S. rule after Spain had transferred their rule of the Philippines to the U.S.
 d. The U.S. withdrew from Cuba.

24. The 1887 General Allotment Act, also known as the Dawes Act, had a policy of giving private property ownership to Native Americans in order to divide the Native American reservations into individual "family farms." What was a practical result of this policy?
 a. Many Native American tribes lost large portions of their reservations.
 b. Many Native Americans became assimilated to the American culture of family farming.
 c. The Nez Perce Conflict occurred between Nez Perce Native Americans and U.S. army forces.
 d. American settlers moved to lands formerly owned by Native Americans and slaughtered most of the buffalo that Native Americans depended on for their livelihood.

Use the excerpt and your knowledge of social studies to answer the following question:
    "Project TRINITY was the name given to the war-time effort [in the United States] to produce the first nuclear detonation. A plutonium-fueled implosion device was detonated on 16 July 1945 at the Alamogordo Bombing Range in south-central New Mexico."
    -from Project Trinity 1945-1946, by Carl Maag and Steve Rohrer

25. Why was Project Trinity a very important program for the U.S. during World War II?
    a. The U.S. wanted to use nuclear energy to power their factories in helping the war effort.
    b. Germany and Japan both had programs to build an atomic bomb, so the U.S. needed one first to win the war.
    c. Italy and Germany both had plans to build an atomic bomb, so the U.S. needed to build one before their enemies did.
    d. The U.S. wanted to use the threat of a nuclear bomb to put down any insurrections that might start in Japanese internment camps in New Mexico.

Use the list and your knowledge of social studies to answer the following question:
    Around 160,000 Allied troops landed along a 50-mile stretch of French coastline to fight Nazi Germany.
    More than 5,000 ships and 13,000 aircraft gave support for the Allied attack.

26. Which World War II battle does the above information describe?
    a. D-day, the Normandy Invasion
    b. Battle of the Bulge
    c. Battle of Midway
    d. Battle of Britain

Use the photograph and your knowledge of social studies to answer the following question:

Some victory gardeners displaying their vegetables 1942 or 1943

27. What was one main purpose of a Victory Garden in the U.S. during World War II?
    a. To ensure that the domestic food supply was not being poisoned by foreign spies or infiltrators
    b. To decrease demand on commercial vegetable growers, making more food available to soldiers
    c. To provide more nutritious food for poor immigrant populations
    d. To sell grown foods at markets and raise money for war bonds

- 82 -

Use the map and your knowledge of social studies to answer the following question:

Post World War II Germany, around 1948-49, showing Germany divided into the American sector, British sector, French sector, and Russian sector. The capital city of Berlin was also divided into those four sectors after the war.

28. This map shows political divisions of Germany after World War II. What else does this map illustrate with the use of arrows?
   a. The area designated as "free airspace" where travelers from the different sectors could travel in between East and West Germany
   b. The "Berlin Bombing" routes used by Allied aircraft to bomb enemy targets in East Berlin that were under control of the U.S.S.R.
   c. The "Berlin Airlift," the routes used by Allied aircraft to airlift supplies to West Berlin because the Soviet Union was imposing a blockade on supplies to West Berlin
   d. The plans for moving Germany's defeated air force and airplanes in between new airports owned by Soviet, American, French, and British governments

Use the list and your knowledge of social studies to answer the following question:
   • Communist North Korea invaded South Korea in 1950.
   • President Truman worried that the Soviet Union and China planned to expand communism throughout Asia.
   • The United Nations passed a resolution in 1950 urging United Nations member countries to give assistance to South Korea in their battle against North Korea.

29. What would be the BEST title for this list that summarizes what all of the items on the list have in common?
   a. Reasons Why the Policy of Containment was Ineffective
   b. Reasons for United States Involvement in the Korean War
   c. Reasons for the Popularity of McCarthyism in the United States
   d. Reasons Why the House Un-American Activities Committee Formed

30. During World War II, Japanese Americans in internment camps were denied the right to be brought before a court to challenge the legality of their imprisonment. This was a violation of which constitutional right?
   a. Right against involuntary servitude
   b. Right to habeas corpus
   c. Right to assemble
   d. Right to vote

31. Which of the following methods was NOT used by suffragettes in their attempt to get the 19th Amendment (allowing women the right to vote) passed?
   a. Marches
   b. Nonviolent protests
   c. Speeches and written articles
   d. Payments to key senators to help the cause

32. The "laissez-faire" economists of the late 1800s, before Progressives had more influence, believed that businesses were best regulated by which entity?
   a. Federal government
   b. State or local governments
   c. Trust-busting laws
   d. Marketplace forces

Use the list and your knowledge of social studies to answer the following question:
   - Provided that shipping rates should be fair and reasonable
   - Required that rate information be made public
   - Outlawed secret rebates
   - Made price discrimination against small markets illegal
   - Promised investigation of any rate abuses

33. The above list shows provisions of which piece of legislation?
   a. Pacific Railway Act of 1862
   b. Interstate Commerce Act of 1887
   c. Dollar Diplomacy Act of 1911
   d. Federal Reserve Act of 1913

34. When President Warren Harding called for a "Return to Normalcy" in 1920, the BEST summary of what he meant would be...

    a. A return to the high employment rate that had dominated the U.S. during World War I

    b. A return to peaceful times and a focus on domestic issues, as opposed to a focus on international war

    c. A return to a period of high immigration rates that were contributing to a diverse culture and growing economy in the U.S.

    d. A return to finding more territories, such as Puerto Rico and Guam acquired during the Spanish-American War, for expanding U.S. markets

35. In the early 1950s, the birthrate in the U.S. kept climbing steadily each year, from around 3.6 million births in 1950 to 4.3 million births in 1957. Which phrase BEST describes this post war phenomenon, and tells an effect of the phenomenon?

    a. "Baby Boom," benefitted the U.S. economy and led to a greater demand for consumer products

    b. "Women Quitting Work Effect," caused an increase in employment opportunities for men

    c. "Soldiers Returning Effect," caused more out-of-wedlock births

    d. "Baby Bust," led to decreased prosperity in the 1950s

Use the list and your knowledge of social studies to answer the following question:

- A Wilderness Protection Act saved forestland from being developed
- The Elementary and Secondary Education Act provided money for public schools
- Medicare was started to help elderly with the costs of health care
- A Housing Act provided money to build low-income housing
- Pollution controls became stronger due to the Air and Water Quality Acts
- Standards were raised for safety in consumer products
- A Food Stamp program was enacted
- Head Start's preschool programs for poor children were created
- The Corporation for Public Broadcasting was created, providing many public television and radio stations

36. All of the programs on the above list fall under what category of programs?

    a. President Franklin D. Roosevelt's New Deal programs

    b. President John F. Kennedy's Civil Rights programs

    c. President Lyndon B. Johnson's Great Society programs

    d. President Richard M. Nixon's American Welfare programs

37. When the Organization of Petroleum Exporting Countries (OPEC) declared an oil embargo against the United States from 1973 to 1974, what was an effect on the U.S. free enterprise system?

    a. Car owners stocked up on gasoline.

    b. Auto manufacturers in the U.S. started selling cars to European customers instead of to U.S. customers.

    c. The effect on the U.S. free enterprise system was minor; the U.S. had stockpiles of oil reserves and was actively drilling for oil in Texas and Alaska.

    d. The U.S. experienced inflation, economic recession, and restrictions on gasoline purchases; auto manufacturers started making smaller and more fuel-efficient cars.

38. In 1997, he was called the "richest man in America" for his approximate net worth of $37 billion, which he earned in the computer industry. He tries to keep the American Dream alive for others by philanthropically donating money to schools, libraries, and computer labs. Who is this American entrepreneur?
    a. Warren Buffett
    b. Bill Gates
    c. Robert Johnson
    d. Sam Walton

Use the excerpt and your knowledge of social studies to answer the following question:
> "The foreman of a Pittsburg coal company may now stand in his subterranean office and talk to the president of the Steel Trust, who sits on the twenty-first floor of a New York skyscraper. The long-distance talks, especially, have grown to be indispensable to the corporations whose plants are scattered and geographically misplaced—to the mills of New England, for instance, that use the cotton of the South and sell so much of their product to the Middle West. To the companies that sell perishable commodities, an instantaneous conversation with a buyer in a distant city has often saved a carload or a cargo."

39. The author of this excerpt is describing the social and economic/business effects of which technological innovation?
    a. Coal smelting
    b. Stock ticker
    c. Telegraph
    d. Telephone

Use the timeline and your knowledge of social studies to answer the following question:
- 1921 - Franklin Roosevelt acquired the disease called polio and lost the use of his legs at age 39
- 1930s - Polio outbreaks became more frequent in the U.S. and public sympathy was high to help the victims
- 1938 - President Franklin Roosevelt founded the National Foundation for Infantile Paralysis (NFIP), later renamed the March of Dimes Foundation, to help fund research for a polio vaccine
- 1955 - Dr. Jonas Salk developed and tested the first successful polio vaccine

40. What is one conclusion that can be made based on this timeline?
    a. Historical events and the specific needs of society can contribute to medical inventions.
    b. Polio outbreaks were worse in the U.S. than in other countries in the 1920s.
    c. A disease outbreak can only be prevented by the development of a vaccine.
    d. Franklin Roosevelt developed the first successful polio vaccine.

Use the chart and your knowledge of social studies to answer the following question:

ERA in U.S. History	Approximate Dates	Defining Characteristics of this Era
Gilded Age or Progressive Era	1890-1914	The era was called "gilded" because of expanded wealth and prosperity. "Progressive" describes the politics of the time that called for social reforms and eliminating corruption in government.
World War I Era	1914-1918	The U.S. was involved in fighting a war in Europe.
Roaring Twenties	1918-1928	
Great Depression	1929-1940	
World War II Era	1941-1945	
Cold War Era	1945-1964	

41. Which defining characteristic listed below should go in the row for describing the Roaring Twenties Era?

a. After a World War, America wanted to help rebuild Europe and prevent the Soviet Union's possible expansion of communism.

b. After the stock market crash, many businesses failed and unemployment became high.

c. The U.S. was involved in fighting a war with Allies against Germany, Japan, and Italy.

d. The economy was strong with a great demand for new products, while culture in this era, also known as the "Jazz Age," became more experimental.

42. Which Founding Father was governor of Connecticut during and after the Revolutionary War, and was the only governor of a British colony who sided with colonists during the Revolutionary War?

a. Charles Carroll

b. Benjamin Rush

c. Jonathan Trumbull

d. John Witherspoon

Use the map and your knowledge of social studies to answer the following question:

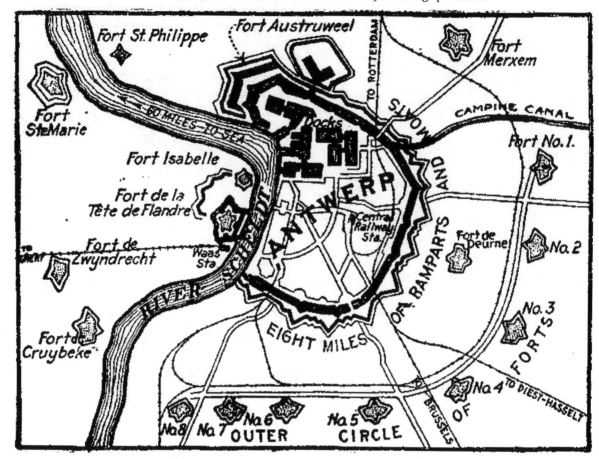

ANTWERP AND ITS FORTIFICATIONS

43. Why was the city of Antwerp in Belgium so heavily fortified in 1914?
    a. World War I had started; Germany had invaded other Belgian cities and was going to invade Antwerp also.
    b. World War I had started; Italy had invaded other Belgian cities and was going to invade Antwerp also.
    c. Antwerp was fortifying against British air attacks that might take place during World War I.
    d. Antwerp feared a Russian invasion after the start of World War I.

44. Which choice below lists some contributions to early America made by John Jay?
    a. He was the first Chief Justice of New York and also a Minister to France.
    b. He signed the Declaration of Independence and was one of the first mayors of New York City.
    c. He served in George Washington's army during the Revolution and was Minister to Spain after the war.
    d. He was a foreign minister, a contributing writer to the Federalist Papers, and an early governor of New York.

- 88 -

Use the photograph, caption, and your knowledge of social studies to answer the following question:

German Air Raiders over England
In the foreground three British planes are advancing to the attack

45. Based on the photograph and caption from a book about World War I, and your general social studies knowledge, which statement below is MOST likely true?
  a. The only airplane warfare during World War I occurred over England.
  b. In World War I, American allies had better airplane technology than German allies.
  c. Airplane warfare was used in the Civil War before being more widely used in World War I.
  d. Airplanes had their first warfare use during World War I, at first just for taking spy photographs, and later for firing guns and dropping bombs.

Use the excerpt and your knowledge of social studies to answer the following question:
  "Perhaps the most characteristic feature of this record of lynch law for the year 1893, is the remarkable fact that five human beings were lynched and that the matter was considered of so little importance that the powerful press bureaus of the country did not consider the matter of enough importance to ascertain the causes for which they were hanged. It tells the world, with perhaps greater emphasis than any other feature of the record,

that Lynch Law has become so common in the United States that the finding of the dead body of a Negro, suspended between heaven and earth to the limb of a tree, is of so slight importance that neither the civil authorities nor press agencies consider the matter worth investigating."

46. The above excerpt comes from a book written by a female African-American "muckraker" journalist and reform leader in 1895. What was this author's name?
    a. Ella Baker
    b. Rosa Parks
    c. Sojourner Truth
    d. Ida B. Wells

Use the excerpt and your knowledge of social studies to answer the following question:
In *The Great Round World and What Is Going On In It*, a weekly magazine, Sanford B. Dole was interviewed in 1898 about the U.S. plan to annex Hawaii:
"President Dole made a glowing picture of the benefits that this country would receive from annexation. It would greatly encourage commerce between the United States and Hawaii by making the trade absolutely free, and it would open up to Americans a great many industries, the chief among them being coffee-growing.
"It would also vastly improve the condition of the islands themselves.
In case annexation is rejected by our Government, President Dole says the Hawaiian Government will continue much as it is at present."

47. What was Sanford B. Dole the president of in 1898?
    a. The Republic of Hawaii
    b. The State of Hawaii
    c. The United States
    d. The United States Senate

Use the list and your knowledge of social studies to answer the following question:
   • It proved that the U.S. was willing to expand its empire and gain resources through imperialism (the taking of colonies).
   • It allowed the U.S. to annex Guam, Hawaii, Puerto Rico, and the Philippines.
   • It showed the power and strength of the U.S. army and navy.

48. What would be the BEST summarizing title for this list?
    a. How the Policies of President Theodore Roosevelt Made the U.S. a World Power
    b. How the Spanish-American War Helped the U.S. Become a World Power
    c. How the War of 1812 Helped the U.S. Become a World Power
    d. How Isolationism Led to Imperialism for the U.S.

Use the excerpt and your knowledge of social studies to answer the following question:
President Woodrow Wilson's "Fourteen Points" speech in 1918 included the following lines:
"XIV. A general association of nations must be formed under specific covenants for the purpose of affording mutual guarantees of political independence and territorial integrity to great and small states alike.

"In regard to these essential rectifications of wrong and assertions of right we feel ourselves to be intimate partners of all the governments and peoples associated together against the Imperialists. We cannot be separated in interest or divided in

49. Based on this excerpt, what was one way that Wilson's "Fourteen Points" contrasted with his pre-war position of U.S. neutrality?
   a. In 1918, Wilson agreed with the philosophy of the imperialists.
   b. By 1918, Wilson thought that each nation should form its own government.
   c. In this speech, Wilson believed that each nation should be able to decide its own territories.
   d. In this speech, Wilson wanted to set up a League of Nations which would eventually become the United Nations.

Use the illustration and your knowledge of social studies to answer the following question:

A sketch from *I Was There...with the Yanks in France* by C. LeRoy Baldridge, written in 1919, shows a sketch of an old trench in the Argonne forest of France

50. Why was the Battle of the Argonne Forest in 1918 difficult and important?
   a. The battle was difficult because there was no air support available to the Allies during this time and important because the Allies won anyway.
   b. The battle was difficult because there were many Allied prisoners of war hidden in the trenches who needed to be rescued and important because the prisoners were rescued.
   c. The battle was difficult because of the deeply forested nature of the area and important because it was the last battle won by the Germans before the end of World War I.
   d. The battle was difficult because the Germans were so entrenched in this forest, having built deep trenches there, and important because it was one of the final battles of the war and helped break through Germany's western front.

51. Progressive Era reformers in the early 1900s wanted greater involvement by federal government in public affairs to improve schools, roads, parks, public health, farms, and more. Because government would need money for such reforms, which amendment did Progressives help pass that allowed income tax collection?
   a. 16th Amendment
   b. 17th Amendment
   c. 18th Amendment
   d. 19th Amendment

52. In the Progressive Era of the late 1890s and early 1900s, political reformers wanted to make sure government represented the peoples' will. An "initiative" process began in 1898 in South Dakota and then spread to other states. Which definition BEST describes the initiative process?
   a. It allowed voting citizens to give their judgment on proposed legislation before state legislators voted on the same legislation.
   b. It allowed voters to gather petitions demanding special elections when they wanted to recall an unpopular public official, thereby allowing them to "un-elect" that official.
   c. It allowed citizens to introduce legislation proposals at a local or state level by gathering petitions, and proposals would then be addressed by lawmakers or placed on ballots for a vote.
   d. It allowed citizens to visit state legislatures and give testimony supporting a certain issue, thereby encouraging the state lawmakers to propose and pass legislation on that same issue.

53. An "Emergency Quota Law" in 1921 was signed by the president to limit new immigrants to the U.S. was most likely an effect of which popular philosophy of the time period?
   a. Harlem Renaissance, which showed that African Americans had much to contribute to society and should be given jobs before letting in more immigrants.
   b. Nativism, a belief that native-born Americans, especially white Americans, were superior to foreign-born Americans.
   c. Prohibition, a belief that alcohol was un-American because beer was mostly brewed by German-Americans, and thus immigration of Germans and other Europeans with alcohol as part of their cultural traditions should be limited.
   d. Women's Suffrage Movement, arguing that women should get rights before more immigrants were let in the U.S.

54. In May 1991, the First International Gathering of Children Hidden during World War II held a meeting in New York City. Around 1,600 former hidden children attended this meeting. Which of the following is the BEST explanation for why these adults had to be hidden as children in Europe during World War II?
    a. They were in danger of being drafted into youth army groups in fascist Germany.
    b. They were hiding from war zones and waiting for fake passports to take them to Israel.
    c. They had to be hidden from French families who would have taken them away from their original homelands to adopt them.
    d. They were Jewish and had to be hidden from Nazis in order to survive the Holocaust, the attempted extermination of the Jewish population by Nazi Germany.

Use the timeline and your knowledge of social studies to answer the following question:
    Dec. 7, 1941 - Pearl Harbor in Hawaii is bombed by Japan. The FBI arrests some Japanese-American community leaders who are held away from their families.

    Dec. 8, 1941 - U.S. Congress declares war on Japan.
    Feb. 19, 1942 - President Franklin D. Roosevelt signs Executive Order 9066, ordering military areas off-limits to certain people.

    March 18, 1942 - President Roosevelt signs Executive Order 9102, which establishes a "War Relocation Authority."

55. What event would BEST go next in this timeline's factual sequence of events?
    a. Thousands of Japanese-American men, women and children are relocated from the U.S. west coast for east coast locations.
    b. All Japanese-American men are denied the chance to be U.S. soldiers for the duration of World War II.
    c. Thousands of Japanese-American men, women and children are relocated to internment camps.
    d. Many Japanese-American men have their passports confiscated and are forced to leave the U.S.

Use the excerpt and your knowledge of social studies to answer the following question:
    "The earnestness of the Americans in the situation was proclaimed to the world by the English and French, and General Pershing placed his name and that of his country and men high on the wall of fame by unselfishly offering to France at the most critical period the use of his entire force, to be disposed of and assigned wherever General Foch and his staff decided to use them. Within a few days thereafter the American troops which had been in training were marched in to relieve the stressed English and French."

56. The author of this excerpt is describing a turning point in which war?
    a. War of 1812
    b. Spanish-American War
    c. World War I
    d. World War II

57. Who headed the National Association for the Advancement of Colored People (NAACP) in 1910, founded and edited the NAACP's journal *The Crisis*, and wrote many "muckraking" articles for *The Crisis* about civil rights for African Americans?
    a. W.E.B. DuBois
    b. Matthew Gaines
    c. Marcus Garvey
    d. Booker T. Washington

58. Which reason or reasons BEST explain why the U.S. Office of War Information included famous stars such as Ethel Merman in their radio broadcasts in the 1940s?
    a. To build morale, raise spirits, and help convince women they needed to stay home while men went to war
    b. To build morale, raise spirits, and help convince women to apply for wartime work
    c. To convince women to buy tickets to Broadway shows to support the U.S. economy during wartime
    d. To convince women to buy movie tickets to support the U.S. economy during wartime

Use the excerpt and your knowledge of social studies to answer the following question:
    "As you know, I will soon be visiting the People's Republic of China and the Soviet Union. I go there with no illusions. We have great differences with both powers. We shall continue to have great differences. But peace depends on the ability of great powers to live together on the same planet despite their differences."

59. Which president gave this speech, as he was about to become the first U.S. President to visit the communist People's Republic of China?
    a. President John F. Kennedy
    b. President Lyndon B. Johnson
    c. President Richard M. Nixon
    d. President Gerald R. Ford

60. What event in April 1975 meant that the Vietnam War was over and that South Vietnam would surrender to the communists, leading to the eventual reunification of the country under communist rule?
    a. Fall of Saigon
    b. Ho Chi Minh's death
    c. My Lai Massacre
    d. Tet Offensive

61. "Old enough to fight, old enough to vote" became a slogan for a youth voting rights movement after the World War II military draft age was lowered to 18, while 21 remained the minimum voting age. The Vietnam War draft brought more urgency to the youth voting rights movement and resulted in which amendment to lower the voting age to 18?
    a. 24th Amendment
    b. 25th Amendment
    c. 26th Amendment
    d. 27th Amendment

Use the list and your knowledge of social studies to answer the following question:

   Poor agricultural practices
   Years of drought
   Lack of ground cover to hold soil in place
   High winds on the plains

62. What would be the BEST title to summarize this list?
   a. Causes of the 1935 Dust Bowl
   b. Effects of the 1935 Dust Bowl
   c. Issues for the 1970s Era Rust Belt
   d. Issues for the 1970s Era Sun Belt

Use the excerpt and your knowledge of social studies to answer the following question:
   Excerpt from *Crossing the Plains, Days of '57* by William Audley Maxwell,
   1915
   "We forded the Platte at a point something like one hundred and fifty miles
   westward from its confluence with the Missouri. There was no road leading
   into the river, nor any evidence of its having been crossed by any one at that
   place. We were informed that the bottom was of quicksand, and fording,
   therefore, dangerous. We tested it, by riding horses across. Contrary to our
   expectations, the bottom was found to be a surface of smooth sand, packed
   hard enough to bear up the wagons, when the movement was quick and
   continuous. A cut was made in the bank, to form a runway for passage of the
   wagons to the water's edge; and the whole train crossed the stream safely,
   with no further mishap than the wetting of a driver and the dipping of a
   wagon into a place deep enough to let water into the box. Fording the Platte
   consumed one entire day. We camped that night on the north shore."

63. Which statement BEST summarizes the main idea of the above paragraph describing
geographic factors for settlers headed to the Great Plains?
   a. Fording the Platte River in stage coach wagons was dangerous because wagons often
   got caught in quicksand
   b. Fording the Platte River was believed to be dangerous, but it turned out to be quick
   and easy for stage coach wagons
   c. Fording the Platte River was thought to be dangerous, but it turned out to be mostly
   time-consuming and a little inconvenient
   d. After fording the Platte River, stage coach wagons could continue driving west or
   could stop and camp for a night by the shore of the river

Use the chart and your knowledge of social studies to answer the following question:
U.S. Census Data
(All population figures are per 200,000 square miles of land area)

Date:	Northeastern U.S. Rural Areas	Northeastern U.S. Urban Areas
1890	Population average of around 7.5 million	Population average of around 12.5 million
1930	Population average of around 11 million	Population average of around 30 million

64. Which conclusion is MOST likely true based on this U.S. Census Data chart?
    a. Rural to urban migration was a probable trend between the years 1890 and 1930.
    b. Urban to rural migration was a probable pattern between the years 1890 and 1930.
    c. Urban areas grew in population numbers but rural areas had a decreased population between 1890 and 1930.
    d. Rural areas grew in population numbers but urban areas had a decreased population between 1890 and 1930.

65. In 1937, President Franklin D. Roosevelt was accused by opponents of trying to "pack the court," and his plan for courts was defeated by the U.S. Senate. What was Roosevelt's plan for the judicial branch at that time?
    a. Roosevelt wanted only Democrats to be appointed to federal district courts
    b. Roosevelt wanted only Democrats to be appointed as Supreme Court justices
    c. Roosevelt wanted to raise the total number of Supreme Court justices from nine to 15
    d. Roosevelt wanted to raise the total number of federal district court judges from 94 to 100

Use the timeline and your knowledge of social studies to answer the following question:
    1962 - The book "Silent Spring," by Rachel Carson, was published and soon became a bestseller. The book exposed the negative effects of pesticides on the environment in the U.S.

    1969 - President Nixon set up a Cabinet-level "Environmental Quality Council" as well as a "Citizens' Advisory Committee on Environmental Quality."

    1970 - In February, President Nixon announced stronger federal programs to deal with water and air pollution.

    1970 - In April that year, the first Earth Day was celebrated in the U.S. by about 20 million Americans.

66. Based on this timeline, which event MOST likely took place in December of 1970?
    a. Future Vice President Al Gore gave a report on global warming to his fellow college students
    b. Vietnam War protests overshadowed the public concern for a healthy environment and the issue faded away for a while
    c. President Nixon oversaw the establishment of the National Park System, setting aside lands for protection and public recreation
    d. President Nixon oversaw the establishment of the Environmental Protection Agency to consolidate pollution control and environmental protection

Question 67 pertains to the following excerpt from *The Black Experience in America*, author Norman Coombs describes a 1960s sit-in:
    "In a matter of weeks, student sit-ins were occurring at segregated lunch counters all across the South. College and high school students by the thousands joined the Civil Rights Movement. These students felt the need to form their own organization to mobilize and facilitate the spontaneous demonstrations which were springing up everywhere."

67. Student "sit-ins" are BEST described as which kind of way to participate in the democratic process?
    a. Displaying Black Power to incite fear
    b. Litigating
    c. Lobbying
    d. Non-violent protesting

Use the excerpt and your knowledge of social studies to answer the following question:
    In this excerpt from *The Black Experience in America*, author Norman Coombs describes 1941 negotiations between civil rights activist A. Philip Randolph, who was planning a March on Washington by African Americans, and President Franklin D. Roosevelt:

    "Finally, Roosevelt contacted Randolph and offered to issue an executive order barring discrimination in defense industries and promised to put "teeth" in the order, provided Randolph call off the march. When Randolph became convinced that Roosevelt's intentions were sincere, he complied.

    Roosevelt fulfilled his promise by issuing Executive Order 8802, which condemned discrimination on the grounds of race, color, or creed. Then, he established the Fair Employment Practices Commission and assigned to it the responsibility for enforcing the order."

68. What conclusion can BEST be made based on this excerpt?
    a. Jobs for African Americans increased during World War II because of manpower needs and because of an anti-discrimination order from the president
    b. Jobs for African Americans increased during World War II because of manpower needs alone, and the anti-discrimination order was probably not really needed
    c. A. Philip Randolph was just bluffing about planning a March on Washington
    d. President Franklin D. Roosevelt was not really worried about African Americans marching on Washington, but he gave in to Randolph's request for an Executive Order anyway

Use the "Cause and Effects" chart and your knowledge of social studies to answer the following question:
    Cause: An important bill is passed in both Congress and the Senate and signed by President Franklin D. Roosevelt in 1944.

    Effect: Men with only high school educations could now go to college.

    Effect: Some of those men became doctors, lawyers, engineers, or joined other middle class professions.

    Effect: The middle class jobs and loans from the same bill allow men to buy houses.

    Effect: Entire suburbs are built with new homes for newly middle class families.

69. Complete this "Cause and Effects" chart by filling in a missing piece of information for "Cause." What was the name of the bill passed in 1944?
    a. Executive Order 9981
    b. G.I. Bill
    c. Smith Act of 1944
    d. Taft-Hartley Act

70. The 1950s included growing income and affluence, a larger middle class, and a baby boom. What other 1950s trend can BEST be considered an effect of those three factors?
    a. Increased consumer spending and consumption
    b. Military-industrial complex
    c. Rock and roll music
    d. The Cold War

71. Power divided between local and central branches of government is a definition of what term?
    a. Bicameralism
    b. Checks and balances
    c. Legislative oversight
    d. Federalism

72. The Senate and the House of Representatives are an example of:
    a. Bicameralism
    b. Checks and balances
    c. Legislative oversight
    d. Federalism

73. The civil rights act that outlawed segregation in schools and public places also:
    a. Gave minorities the right to vote
    b. Established women's right to vote
    c. Outlawed unequal voter registration
    d. Provided protection for children

74. Which court case established the Court's ability to overturn laws that violated the Constitution?
    a. Miranda v. Arizona
    b. Marbury v. Madison
    c. United States v. Curtiss-Wright Export Corporation
    d. Brown v. Board of Education of Topeka

75. The first ten amendments to the Constitution are more commonly known as:
    a. The Civil Rights Act
    b. Common law
    c. The Equal Protection clause
    d. The Bill of Rights

76. Which Supreme Court case enforced the civil rights of citizens to not incriminate themselves?
    a. Marbury v. Madison
    b. Miranda v. Arizona
    c. Youngstown Sheet and Tube Company v. Sawyer
    d. United States v. Carolene Products Company

77. What judicial system did America borrow from England?
    a. Due process
    b. Federal law
    c. Commerce law
    d. Common law

78. The writers of The Federalist Papers published under the pen name "Publius." Who were the authors?
    a. James Madison, John Jay, and Alexander Hamilton
    b. George Washington, Thomas Jefferson, and James Madison
    c. Alexander Hamilton, Benjamin Franklin, and Thomas Jefferson
    d. Benjamin Franklin, John Jay, and Thomas Jefferson

79. To be President of the United States, one must meet these three requirements:
    a. The President must be college educated, at least 30 years old, and a natural citizen
    b. The President must be a natural citizen, have lived in the U.S. for 14 years, and have a college education
    c. The President must be a natural citizen, be at least 35 years old, and have lived in the U.S. for 14 years
    d. The President must be at least 30 years old, be a natural citizen, and have lived in the U.S. for 14 years

80. The President may serve a maximum of _____ according to the ___ Amendment.
    a. Three four-year terms; 23rd
    b. Two four-year terms; 22nd
    c. One four-year term; 22nd
    d. Two four-year terms; 23rd

81. Senators were originally chosen by state legislatures. In what year was the constitution amended to allow for them to be elected by popular vote?
    a. 1826
    b. 1891
    c. 1913
    d. 1935

82. Who may write a bill?
    a. Anyone
    b. A member of the House
    c. A Senator
    d. Any member of Congress

83. Congressional elections are held every _____ years.
   a. Four
   b. Two
   c. Six
   d. Three

84. How is a tie broken in the Senate?
   a. The President Pro Tempore casts the deciding vote
   b. The Speaker of the House votes
   c. They vote again
   d. The Vice President votes

85. A newly introduced bill is first given to a _____ where it is either accepted, amended or rejected completely.
   a. Full committee
   b. Conference committee
   c. Subcommittee
   d. Senate committee

86. Most state governments have a bicameral legislature. Which one of the following states does not?
   a. Utah
   b. Nebraska
   c. Washington
   d. Louisiana

87. What does the 10th Amendment establish?
   a. Any power not given to the federal government belongs to the states, or the people
   b. The President is responsible for executing and enforcing laws created by Congress
   c. Congress has the authority to declare war
   d. The Supreme Court has the authority to interpret the Constitution

88. Parks and recreation services, police and fire departments, housing services, emergency medical services, municipal courts, transportation services, and public works usually fall under the jurisdiction of which body of government?
   a. State government
   b. Federal government
   c. Federal agencies
   d. Local government

89. How is the jurisdiction of federal courts usually decided?
   a. By the President
   b. By Congress
   c. By the voters
   d. By the Supreme Court

90. How must inferior courts interpret the law?
    a. According to the Supreme Court's interpretation
    b. According to the Constitution
    c. However they choose
    d. According to the political climate

91. What would be considered an informal qualification for being elected President?
    a. The President must be well-traveled
    b. The President must be at least 40 years old
    c. The President must have good character
    d. The President must be a natural citizen

92. How is a tie in the Electoral College broken to choose the President?
    a. Each state's delegation in the House of Representatives gets a vote, and the majority wins
    b. Each state's delegation in the Senate gets a vote, and the majority wins
    c. The former Vice President becomes President
    d. The Speaker of the House casts the deciding vote

93. Which of the following statements about the House is true?
    a. The House does not approve appointments or ratify treaties
    b. Every member of the House of Representatives is given one vote
    c. The members of the House are elected every three years
    d. The House must approve appointments of the Vice Presidency and any treaty involving foreign trade

94. Which constitutional requirement for passing a bill rarely happens?
    a. The leader of the majority party decides when to place the bill on the calendar for consideration before Congress
    b. The versions of a bill that pass through both houses of Congress and are signed by the President must have the exact same wording
    c. The number and kind of amendments introduced in the House are limited
    d. A filibuster needs a supermajority vote to be broken

95. How many members of the Electoral College represent Washington, D.C.?
    a. One
    b. Two
    c. Three
    d. Five

96. Special interest groups are considered experts in certain public policy:
    a. Definitions
    b. Processes
    c. Implementation
    d. Areas

97. Authoritarian regimes often have which type of legislature?
   a. Bicameral
   b. Unicameral
   c. Multi-cameral
   d. Representative

98. What does nationalism accomplish?
   a. Nationalism legitimizes authority and establishes unity
   b. Nationalism creates chaos
   c. Nationalism causes division
   d. Nationalism causes people to question their leaders

99. What kind of nation is made up of special interest groups focused on the civil liberties influencing public policy?
   a. Fascist
   b. Communist
   c. Pluralist
   d. Socialist

100. What do Marxists and capitalists have in common?
   a. They both believe in privatizing land ownership
   b. They both support free international trade
   c. They both support nationalization of the private sector
   d. They both support special interest groups

101. How do banks create money?
   a. By printing it
   b. By taking it out of the Federal Reserve
   c. By loaning it out
   d. By putting it into the Federal Reserve
   e. All of the above

102. Which of the following is a supply shock likely to produce?
   I.   An increase in input prices
   II.   An increase in price levels
   III. A decrease in employment
   IV.   A decrease in GDP
   a. I and III only
   b. II and IV only
   c. I, II, and III only
   d. I, II, III, and IV
   e. None of the above

103. Which of the following correctly states the equation of exchange?
   a. $MV = PQ$
   b. $MP \times VQ$
   c. MP / VQ
   d. $VP = MQ$
   e. $1/MP = VQ$

104. John Maynard Keynes advocated what?
   a. Supply-side economics
   b. Demand-side economics
   c. Laissez faire economics
   d. The Laffer Curve
   e. Say's Law

105. How is the long-run Phillips curve different than the short-run Phillips curve?
   a. In the long-run Phillips curve, there is a trade-off between unemployment and inflation
   b. In the long-run Phillips curve, unemployment is always greater than inflation
   c. In the long-run Phillips curve, there is no trade-off between unemployment and inflation
   d. In the long-run Phillips curve, unemployment equals inflation
   e. In the long-run Phillips curve, there is no such thing as unemployment

106. Which of the following is most likely to benefit from inflation?
   a. A bond investor who owns fixed-rate bonds
   b. A retired widow with no income other than fixed Social Security payments
   c. A person who has taken out a fixed-rate loan
   d. A local bank who has loaned money out at fixed rate
   e. All of the above

107. How does unionized labor in an industry typically affect the wages of workers in that industry during a downturn in the economy when AD decreases?
   a. It makes wages more likely to change
   b. It makes wages more "sticky"
   c. It has no effect on wages; instead, it causes AS to decrease
   d. It has no effect on wages; instead, it causes AS to increase
   e. All of the above

108. Assume a nation's economy is in recession. The nation has an MPC of 0.9 and the government wants to enact fiscal policy to shift the AD curve by $10 billion dollars. What must the government do to its current spending rate?
   a. Decrease spending by $10 billion
   b. Increase spending by $10 billion
   c. Decrease spending by $1 billion
   d. Increase spending by $1 billion
   e. Increase spending by $20 billion

109. Assume that Guatemala has a surplus in its capital account. What might this mean?
   a. It must also have a surplus in its current account
   b. The value of Guatemalan goods bought by foreigners is greater than the value of foreign goods bought by Guatemalans
   c. Its balance of payments must be unequal
   d. The value of foreign goods bought by Guatemalans is greater than the value of Guatemalan goods bought by foreigners
   e. None of the above

110. The price of gasoline skyrockets, dramatically affecting the amount that producers spend to send their goods to market. What do you expect to happen in the short run?
    a. Prices increase, GDP increases
    b. Prices decrease, GDP decreases
    c. Prices increase, GDP decreases
    d. Prices decrease, GDP increases
    e. Prices stay the same, GDP stays the same

111. Thrifty Buy More sells blue baseball hats at $10 a hat in May. The equilibrium price for blue baseball hats increases to $12 in June. Which of the following is a potential explanation for the change?
    a. An increase in supply of blue baseball hats
    b. A decrease in demand for blue baseball hats
    c. Both supply and demand stay the same
    d. Government subsides make it less costly to produce blue hats
    e. Substitute goods decrease in supply

112. Which of the following examples illustrates the law of diminishing marginal utility?
    a. When the price of a good increases from $10 to $12, Bob demands less of the good
    b. As the supply of a good increases, consumers demand less of the good
    c. As Juan buys more units of a single good, he gets less satisfaction from each new purchase
    d. As Sally's income decreases, she is forced to reconsider the goods and services she buys
    e. As a consumer's income decreases, the total utility he or she derives from that income, measured in utils, also decreases

113. Assume you've invested $1,000,000 to begin a business. At the end of the year, revenues equal $1,200,000. During that same year, you could have worked for $300,000. Which of the following statements is true?
    a. Accounting profit equals $200,000
    b. Economic profit equals accounting profit
    c. Accounting profit equals $300,000
    d. Economic profit equals $500,000
    e. The economic profit is greater than the accounting profit

114. What does the distinctive, outwardly bowed shape of the PPF signify?
    a. The law of supply and demand
    b. The efficiency of the free market system
    c. That the two goods do not have constant opportunity costs when producing in different quantities along the PPF.
    d. The unequal distribution of wealth within a society
    e. The shift in demand to match a corresponding shift in supply

Use the following statements to answer Question 115:
  I. Increase supply of labor
  II. Decrease supply of labor
  III. Increase wage earned by labor
  IV. Decrease wage earned by labor

115. How will a labor union affect a labor market?
    a. I and III only
    b. I and IV only
    c. II and III only
    d. II and IV only
    e. None of the above

To answer question 116, consider the following short-run data for Bob's Widgets, a perfectly competitive firm:
    Total Revenue: $100
    Total Costs: $200
    Total Fixed Costs: $90
    Total Variable Costs: $110

116. What should Bob's do?
    a. Increase production
    b. Decrease production but continue to produce
    c. Lower fixed costs
    d. Shut down
    e. None of the above

117. Which of the following statements about public goods is true?
    a. The free market excels in producing them
    b. When a person uses the good, it prevents others from using the good
    c. There is no demand for public goods
    d. It is difficult to prevent people from using the good without paying
    e. They are equally valued by all people

118. Which of the following statements is true about an oligopoly?
    a. There are no or very few barriers to entry
    b. Many firms participate
    c. Collusion may be planned or unplanned
    d. The demand curve is straight
    e. Economies of scale are limited or nonexistent

119. Short-run production is the time period during which _____. Long-run production is the time period during which _____.
    a. a company's profits are maximized; a company's profits can be made greater
    b. a company's costs are fixed; a company's costs can be decreased
    c. a plant's revenue is fixed; a plant's revenue can increase
    d. a company's production will not change; a company's production will change
    e. a plant's production capacity cannot be changed; a plant's production capacity can be changed

Consider the following statements to answer Question 120:
- I. Supply and demand
- II. What goods and services will be produced?
- III. How goods and services will be produced
- IV. To which people will goods be distributed?

120. Which basic questions do all economic systems need to answer?
a. I only
b. I, II, and III
c. II and IV
d. II, III, and IV
e. IV only

Answers and Explanations

1. B: The Pecos River is in New Mexico and Texas, emptying into the Rio Grande. The Red River (A) is a major Oklahoma river running along the Oklahoma–Texas border. The Canadian River (C) is a major Oklahoma river running through the middle of the state, entering from Texas south of the Oklahoma panhandle at the western border, dipping south at the state's center, then moving north to the middle, through Eufaula Lake to the east, and joining with the Arkansas River (D), another major Oklahoma river that enters the state at its northern border east of center and heads southeast out of the state into Arkansas at Oklahoma's eastern border, slightly south of the middle.

2. C: Arcadia Lake is north-northeast of Oklahoma City, and Lake Thunderbird is south-southeast of Oklahoma City; both are the closest lakes to the city. Lake Eufaula, a very large lake, is east and south of Oklahoma City, on Route 40 and south of it, and also on Routes 69 and 270; Sardis Lake is southeast of Lake Eufaula (A). Lake Texoma is far south-southeast of the city at the state's southern border on Routes 35 and 69; Atoka Lake is southeast of Oklahoma City and northeast of Lake Texoma near Route 69 (B). Tom Steed Lake is directly north of Altus and Route 62, southwest of Oklahoma City; Lake Altus-Lugert is west-northwest of Tom Steed Lake and Altus (D).

3. A: From 1900 to 1930, Oklahoma's employment increased from 266,000 to 828,000, more than triple. Its population also increased more than three times—from 790,000 to 2,396,000, but not four times (B). While agriculture continued to be the state's primary activity, it did not grow more during this time (C): It decreased, from 70 to 37 percent of the state's employment. Oklahoma's natural resources, including petroleum, cattle, and cotton, contributed to the majority of new manufacturing industry, like oil refineries, meat-packing plants, and cotton gins (D).

4. D: Sequoyah was born in Tennessee (A) in 1776. He moved in his youth to Georgia and then to Alabama, was a delegate to the federal government from Arkansas, and went from Oklahoma to Texas and Mexico in 1842 to aid the Cherokee, dying from the trip (B). In Alabama, he fought in the War of 1812 for the United States, against the Creek Indians (C) and British troops. After learning to write English from a white farmer in Georgia, he began developing a Cherokee writing system in 1809. After the War of 1812, he invented the 85-letter Talking Leaves Cherokee written alphabet (D), a phonetic system that the Cherokee Nation adopted in 1821. Because of Sequoyah's contribution, thousands of Cherokee achieved literacy within months of its adoption, enabling them to record history; read military orders; write letters; and publish newspapers, educational materials, religious brochures, and legal documents.

5. D: Parker, initially a brilliant Comanche warrior and military strategist, began by fighting white encroachment on Indian Territory, notably in the Battle of Adobe Walls. But realistically knowing the white man's greater population and weaponry would annihilate the Comanche, he advised them to disarm and "take the white man's road" (B). He became a successful rancher and farmer; a leading diplomat, representing the Comanche in Congress; an astute businessman and major stockholder in the Quanah, Acme, and Pacific Railway, who generated prosperity for the Comanche through leasing grazing land and investments in tribal cattle herds, other ranching, schools, and houses; president of his local school

board; judge in the Court of Indian Offenses; and an influential medicine man and religious leader, helping establish the Native American Church and fighting for Indian religious freedom. He combined adapting to white culture and achieving Comanche–white peace with preserving his cultural heritage (C).

6. C: Of the Kiowa Five,* whose art gained fame in eastern white America, Jack Hokeah later inspired numerous artists in Santa Fe, New Mexico, for 10 years. Monroe Tsatoke (A) painted a series of murals on the walls of the Oklahoma Historical Society's third floor in Oklahoma City. Stephen Mopope (B) later painted murals depicting pre-Oklahoma statehood Kiowa life on the walls of the Anadarko Post Office building, sponsored by FDR's Works Project Administration (WPA) project; Kiowa Five members Spencer Asah and James Auchiah (D) assisted him. Today, these murals still exist. *Note: The Kiowa Five were actually six, Lois Smokey being the sixth member. Though her work was included in most of the early Kiowa artists' exhibits, and while all six were students at Oklahoma University, her parents rented a large house in Norman where they all lived; she was subsequently overlooked in the credit given the others for Native American art.

7. D: After being Cherokee deputy chief for two years, Mankiller became the Cherokee Nation's first woman principal chief in 1985, reelected in 1987 and 1991, serving for 10 years (A). She was popular and might have been reelected in 1995 but did not run due to poor health. She worked to improve Cherokee health care, educational, and governmental systems and was also a women's rights activist (B). She published books on history; state–tribal diplomacy; a traditional Cherokee cookbook; her autobiography, *Mankiller: A Chief and Her People* (1993); coauthored *Every Day Is a Good Day: Reflections by Contemporary Indigenous Women* (2004) with a foreword by her close friend feminist leader Gloria Steinem; and taught for three months in 1996 at Dartmouth College (C). She received many awards, including the Presidential Medal of Freedom in 1998; after her 2010 death, President Obama honored her (D) for having "transformed the nation-to-nation relationship between the Cherokee Nation and the federal government" and inspiring women nationwide.

8. B: The Louisiana Purchase acquired the territory that is now Oklahoma in 1803. The Oklahoma Panhandle was ceded to the Spanish government in return for Florida Territory (A) in 1819 through the Adams–Onís Treaty. The Indian Removal Act forced Seminole tribes to relocate to Indian Territory (C) in 1830, triggering the Seminole Wars in 1835. Anticipating admission of Oklahoma as a state to the Union, Congress formally designated Indian Territory and Oklahoma Territory through the Oklahoma Organic Act (D) in 1890 to establish organized incorporated U.S. territories. During the following 16 years, Congress passed a series of laws to unite the Indian and Oklahoma Territories into one state.

9. D: As the Civil War began, in 1861, the United States withdrew military troops from Oklahoma's Indian Territory as Texas troops moved northward. Confederates and all major Indian tribes signed alliance treaties. An Indian delegate was sent to the Confederate Congress in Richmond, Virginia, representing the Indian Territories. But, the South was opposed by some minorities, continuing the fighting within Oklahoma's Indian Territory. Once Union troops controlled Arkansas bordering Oklahoma, it was not long before Union forces, supported by pro-Union Indians, invaded the territory, winning a strategic victory at Honey Springs in 1863. Many pro-Confederate Indians fled south. But Brigadier General Stand Watie, who was Cherokee, continued the Southern rebellion until the end of the war, becoming the last Confederate general to surrender in June of 1865.

10. D: Oklahoma became the 46th state in America in 1907. The year 1900 (A) saw more than 30 Indian tribes relocated to what were the Indian Territories, while Texas ranchers began moving in, seeking new pasture. Settlers who crossed the borders ahead of government permission were called Sooners, which became the state nickname. In 1902 (B), Indian Territory tribal leaders attempted to form their own state, called Sequoyah. They held the Sequoyah Constitutional Convention in 1905 (C). They petitioned Congress with overwhelming residential support, but Congress, wanting to join the Indian and Oklahoma Territories into one state, rejected the idea of separate statehood for each.

11. B: The Five Civilized Indian Nations (Cherokee, Chickasaw, Choctaw, Creek, and Seminole) brought big herds of cattle with them when they were resettled from the southeastern United States to Oklahoma's Indian Territory in the 1830s. They practiced communal land ownership, enabling open-range grazing. Without an immediate market, herd sizes grew. During the 1850s, the California Gold Rush created great demand for cattle, (C) further spurring the Indians to raise more stock. The chaos of the Civil War and raids by cattle thieves caused the Indians to lose roughly 300,000 head of cattle (A). Following the war, the great cattle drives from Texas began in 1867; the Chisholm and Western Trails both crossed Oklahoma, creating an economic boom (D). Though Cherokee leaders and cattlemen were against it, the U.S. government ordered the Cherokee Outlet Opening in 1893 to allow white settlement, removing cattle herds and ending open-range grazing (B).

12. A: In 1910, immigrants comprised 40,000 of Oklahoma's population, equaling more than 2 percent. While a small proportion of the state, they significantly influenced Oklahoma settlement, with evidence of this remaining to this day. In Pittsburg County's coal fields at the turn of the 20th century, a large population of miners had come from Italy and Poland, not Germany or Russia (B). German Mennonites, however, had migrated from their homes in Russia to the western Oklahoma area of the Washita River (C). In north-central Oklahoma, the city of Enid had a large ethnic community of Germans, not Czechs (D). However, elsewhere in north-central Oklahoma, particularly in Oklahoma County, Lincoln County, and Garfield County, Czech immigrants did settle. Today, Krebs' Italian restaurants, Harrah's Polish store names, Yukon's Czech festival, and Oklahoma City's German classes and bilingual services at a church are evidence of European immigrant legacies.

13. B: Oklahoma agriculture had not been booming before the Great Depression (A); it had been suffering for the 10 years before 1930. These difficulties were exacerbated by the regional drought in Oklahoma that year. At the same time, the East Texas oil field opened, providing a surplus of oil (C). This created a glut on the petroleum market, making oil prices plummet, which in turn caused widespread layoffs of oil-rig employees. Joblessness became so serious that Oklahoma City and Tulsa both formed unemployment committees by the end of 1930. The economy of Oklahoma hit bottom during the winter of 1932 and 1933 (D). (The period of 1935 to 1936 was during FDR's New Deal, which though it did not pull Oklahoma out of the Depression, did bring many positive benefits to the state.)

14. A: When Oklahoma became a U.S. state in 1907, it included prohibition in its state constitution, 10 years before the government passed wartime prohibition in 1917 during World War I (B). That same year, Congress passed resolutions for the 18th Amendment for prohibition. The first states to ratify the 18th Amendment (C) in 1918 were Arizona, Delaware, Florida, Georgia, Kentucky, Louisiana, Maryland, Massachusetts, Mississippi, Montana, North Dakota, South Carolina, South Dakota, Texas, and Virginia; Connecticut

voted against it. The second group ratifying it in 1919 included Alabama, Arkansas, California, Colorado, Idaho, Illinois, Indiana, Iowa, Kansas, Maine, Michigan, Missouri, Nebraska, New Hampshire, North Carolina, Ohio, Oklahoma, Oregon, Tennessee, Utah, Washington, West Virginia, and Wyoming. This equaled the required number of states, making prohibition a law on January 16, 1919. However, these additional states ratified the amendment from January 17 through February 25, after the fact (D): Minnesota, New Mexico, Nevada, New York, Pennsylvania, Vermont, and Wisconsin; Rhode Island voted against it.

15. A: Originally, native grasses held the Great Plains fine-textured soil in place. The Great Plains were overgrazed by herds of cattle and sheep. Then European settlers, coming to farm under the U.S. Homestead Act, brought traditional farming methods with them, for example, deep plowing. In addition, mechanized plowing and harvesting technologies enabled large-scale agriculture. Crop prices were raised by the effects of the Russian Revolution and World War I together, spurring widespread land cultivation. In addition to deep plowing's eliminating grasses, cotton farmers left their fields unplanted over the winter during the High Plains' windiest season and burned plant stubble before planting to inhibit weeds, depleting organic nutrients and surface growth. These practices made the soil vulnerable to erosion, which attacked the land after a severe 1930 drought. Droughts recurred in 1934, 1936, and 1939 to 1940, though some High Plains areas had drought conditions continuing up to eight years. The first drought caused crop failure, exposing fields to wind erosion and leading to dust storms so severe that they often reduced visibility to zero during the Dust Bowl.

16. B: Tulsa's first oil boom was from 1901 to 1907. Oil discovered in Red Fork in 1901 transformed Tulsa from a small frontier town into a boomtown. The Glenn Pool oil field, discovered in 1905, ultimately established Tulsa as the petroleum industry's center and Oklahoma as a primary American petroleum producer. Following Oklahoma's 1907 statehood, refineries were constructed in and around Tulsa. Another wave of 1915 to 1930 oil strikes established Tulsa as the oil capital of the world. The population expanded, and the city thrived, with prominent architectural and cultural development. Though the Great Depression halted further population growth, it did not damage Tulsa's economy, as in most Midwestern areas. The decades 1940 through 1960 saw ongoing prosperity, not an oil bust (C); Tulsa was America's most beautiful city. The decades 1960 through 1980 were a period of urban renewal, not an oil bust (D): Tulsa was the first major Oklahoma city initiating such a program. The oil bust was from 1982 to 1984, when Houston overtook Tulsa as oil capital of the world. Tulsa leaders diversified the city's economy to aviation, telecommunications, Internet, factory jobs, and also natural gas during its recovery period to date.

17. D: Jim Crow laws covered all these areas from 1890 to 1957 but, from 1954 to 1957, were commonest regarding public accommodations, miscegenation, and adoption. For example, a 1954 statute required separate restrooms in mines; a 1955 statute prohibited black–white intermarriage, penalized by up to $500 and one to five years in prison; and a 1957 statute required adoption petitions to identify the child's and petitioners' races. Statutes regarding education and voting rights were common from the 1890s until *Brown v. Board of Education* prohibited educational segregation in 1954; and while the 15th Amendment granted black men voting rights in 1870, 1907 Oklahoma statutes prohibited indigent and illiterate persons from voting, exempting those enfranchised by 1866 and their descendants. The latter was declared unconstitutional in 1915, but its literacy provision was upheld. A 1908 statute decreed segregated railroad coaches (B). A 1925 city ordinance

segregated entertainers (bands and boxers); a 1937 statute segregated public carriers; and a 1949 statute ordered a segregated health care institution for disabled or orphaned black children (C). Hence, (A) is inaccurate.

18. A: The Tulsa Race Riot occurred in 1921 in America's wealthiest black community, Greenwood, the Black Wall Street, burning it to the ground. A 1916 Tulsa ordinance (A) mandated residential segregation, though the U.S. Supreme Court declared this unconstitutional. As returning soldiers reentered the labor market, black World War I veterans demanded their civil rights; across the North and Midwest, many white immigrants, competing for employment with blacks, frequently led race riots during 1919's Red Summer (B). The Ku Klux Klan expanded in cities nationwide after 1915. However, the KKK's first major Oklahoma appearance was two to three months after the Tulsa Race Riot (C). Over unproven assault rumors with no charges pressed, whites formed an apparent lynch mob. The sheriff and police protected the accused, particularly after a 1920 lynching. He fled to his mother's house in Greenwood. Some black men armed themselves to support officials. Armed whites and blacks converged on the courthouse; shots were fired (D). Black Greenwood residents retreated, pursued by an armed white mob. The state National Guard and American Legion became involved. Following continued gunfire, the white mob set fires the next day. Air attacks, vandalism, casualties, martial law, and more ensued. Legal system corruption and cover-ups thwarted reparations.

19. D: In *Guinn v. United States,* the Supreme Court struck down a grandfather clause exempting white voters from a literacy test required of black voters in 1915 (A). Oklahoma then passed a voter registration law in 1916 requiring citizens who had not voted in 1914 to register to vote in 11 days or lose their voting rights. In *Lane v. Wilson,* the Supreme Court invalidated this law in 1939 (B). In *Sipuel v. Board of Regents of University of Oklahoma,* the Supreme Court required Oklahoma to admit a black woman into law school in 1948 (C). After two Supreme Court sessions, with Thurgood Marshall's leadership, the state gave Sipuel a one-person "law school" with two professors, using the State Capitol library. Sipuel returned to state court, arguing this separate-but-equal treatment did not meet Supreme Court standards, still applying to the law school. Eventually, the university president ordered her admission, but she and other black students were segregated. While Sipuel was still there, *McLaurin v. Oklahoma State Regents* remedied this in 1950 (D): The Court ruled segregation removed a graduate student's rights to equal protection under the law, setting precedent for Brown *v. Board of Education* with public schools in 1954.

20. D: Gary became governor of Oklahoma in 1955. One of his first acts upon assuming office was to order the removal of the whites-only and colored-Only signs from the restrooms in the Oklahoma State Capitol (A). He also announced in a statewide radio address that he intended to ensure Oklahoma's compliance with the U.S. Supreme Court ruling in *Brown v. Board of Education,* declaring public school segregation unconstitutional and saying he would not tolerate or defend any school board's defiance of the decision. He further demonstrated his support of the law by getting an amendment passed to the Oklahoma state constitution to eliminate financing of segregated schools. This was unpopular for the time and place. A white Southern Baptist, Gary said, according to his son Jerdy, "You know, this is the right thing to do. We're all God's children, and that's what we're going to do." Before being elected governor, Gary was an Oklahoma state senator from 1941 to 1955, so (C) is not true.

21. C: The Populist movement arose in the U.S. in the 1890s as a grassroots political movement started by southern and western farmers to fight banks, railroads, large corporations and other "elites." "Farmers United" sounds like it could be a correct choice, given the involvement of farmers, but it is incorrect. Choice A and D are also incorrect, although the "Social Gospel" movement was active around the same time period. Entrepreneurship was also on the rise during that time period.

22. A: There has not yet been an era in U.S. History defined by a land form (for example, something like a "Rocky Mountain Era"). There was a Gold Rush era but that was not named specifically for a land form. So A is the BEST choice. There have been eras defined by wars (Civil War Era), economic growth or failure (Roaring Twenties, Great Depression), and by social reforms (Progressive Era).

23. B: The sinking of the USS Maine happened in 1898, and the fact that America blamed Spain was a major cause of the U.S. and Spain declaring war on each other in 1898. All the other events listed did not happen in 1898, so even though they are related to the Spanish-American War, they would not be the correct answer. Choice A happened in 1895, choice C occurred in 1899, and choice D happened in 1902.

24. A: Choice D sounds like a good option, because this is something that did happen, but it happened before the Dawes Act. The Nez Perce conflict of 1877 also occurred before the Dawes Act, so choice C is incorrect. Choice B was the hope of Dawes and other American politicians who planned the act in order to try to help "assimilate" Native Americans, but that was not the practical result as much as choice A, the taking over of reservation lands away from Native Americans.

25. B: Germany and Japan both had scientists working on nuclear bombs, and one of Project Trinity's most important goals was to make sure that the U.S. developed a bomb first and could thereby win the war through superior technology. Italy was not yet working on atomic bombs. A student might pick choice D because the excerpt mentions New Mexico and potential Japanese enemies, but that is incorrect. Choice A is also incorrect as the development of nuclear energy was not the goal of Project Trinity.

26. A: The "French coastline" is a clue that the Normandy Invasion is the correct answer, although a student may think "Bulge" or "Midway" is located in France. The high number of troops, ships, and aircraft is another clue that the facts describe D-Day. But a student not familiar with all of the other battles in World War II may pick one of the incorrect answers.

27. B: A main purpose of Victory Gardens was to decrease demand on commercial vegetable growers, thereby making more food available to soldiers. There were other purposes, such as providing nutritious foods to all people (not just poor immigrants) on the home front and boosting morale at home, but those were secondary and are not listed as answer choices. The other three answer choices listed are all incorrect.

28. C: The map's arrows show the routes the Berlin Airlift used to supply West Berlin with food supplies during a Soviet blockade. It does not show a bombing route, a route for moving captured German airplanes, or a route for tourists.

29. B: While all the titles have a connection of some kind to at least one or two items on the given list, choice B provides the BEST title for the list to show what all the items have in

common: reasons for U.S. involvement in the Korean War. The policy of containment may have been partially effective, because Korea was only one country falling to communism. The United Nations item would probably not fall under a title about containment, McCarthyism, or the HUAC committee, because those were all more internal to the U.S. only. The U.N. was encouraging nations to get involved in the Korean War, so it fits under that title.

30. B: Students who know the meaning of "right to habeas corpus" will know that it means the right to be brought before a court, which was unconstitutionally denied to Japanese Americans in internment camps during World War II. The other options are all rights which were also violated against Japanese Americans in camps, but not in this particular example of not getting a court date. A student who does not know the meaning of *habeas corpus* may be able to use process of elimination about the other rights (although they may confuse "assembling" with going to a court, or confuse "involuntary servitude" with camp "imprisonment") in order to get the correct answer.

31. D: Payments to senators were not a method used by suffragettes trying to get the 19th Amendment allowing women the right to vote passed. They did use all of the other methods, however, such as speeches, writing articles, nonviolent protesting, and marching.

32. D: It is the best description of what laissez-faire economists believed, which is that marketplace forces were enough to regulate businesses. In contrast, most Progressives wanted more trust-busting laws and federal, state, and local government intervention to help regulate businesses that were perhaps producing unsafe products, forming monopolies to drive up prices, or taking advantage of working people.

33. B: The Interstate Commerce Act of 1887 provided for all the measures listed in the table, although not all were able to be completely enforced. Reading the list carefully and having a general knowledge of social studies and U.S. history should lead students to the correct answers, although a student could mistakenly pick one of the other choices listed for their connection to railways, dollars, or Federal Reserve money. (Dollar Diplomacy was a strategy, not an actual piece of legislation.)

34. B: It is the BEST summary for what President Warren Harding meant by a "Return to Normalcy." He was calling for a return to peaceful times and a focus on domestic issues, as opposed to a focus on international war. Choice A is a good guess because the president would want a good economy, and industry had been busy during WWI before falling off slightly after the war. But choice B is the best answer. He was not calling for going out in search of more territories or for higher immigration rates.

35. A: While an argument could be made that choice B is also correct, there was not a phenomenon actually named the "Women Quitting Work Effect," so choice A is the BEST choice for describing the phenomenon illustrated by the given statistic. The statistic shows the post war Baby Boom, and its effect was to increase the economy and consumer demand for products. Choice D describes the opposite of a Baby Boom, so it is not correct, and choice C was not a historical phenomenon.

36. C: All the programs listed were part of President Lyndon B. Johnson's Great Society programs. The students' general knowledge of social studies should place most of those programs within the 1960s time period, making Presidents Kennedy or Johnson the best

guesses. But because many of the programs do not have to do with civil rights, Johnson becomes the best guess for a student to make over the other choices provided.

37. D: The result of OPEC's oil embargo on the U.S. free enterprise system was inflation, economic recession, and restrictions on gasoline purchases; and auto manufacturers making smaller and more fuel-efficient cars. U.S. auto manufacturers may have sold cars to Europe also, but Europe was also targeted by OPEC's embargo. Choices A and C are also incorrect.

38. B: While all the entrepreneurs listed are also philanthropic donors, and have at times been considered one of the richest men in the world, the mention of "computer industry" will be a clue to most students with basic social studies/current events knowledge that Bill Gates is the correct answer.

39. D: The stock ticker and the telegraph could be related to the information in this excerpt because they were ways for businessmen to relay information to each other, as described in the excerpt. However, the astute student will see that the excerpt describes businessmen talking to each other, therefore the excerpt is describing the benefits of the telephone invention. A student might pick choice A, coal smelting, if they only focus on the first sentence of the excerpt about the coal company foreman.

40. A: It can BEST be made based on the timeline facts. Historical events and the specific needs of society can contribute to medical inventions, such as how the history of polio outbreaks and the fact that a President had the disease contributed to the scientific discovery of a polio vaccine. The other statements cannot be proven true by the timeline facts. Other countries besides the U.S. also had polio outbreaks in the 1920s and 1930s. Disease outbreaks can sometimes be prevented in other ways besides just from vaccines. And it was Jonas Salk, not FDR, who invented the polio vaccine, although FDR helped raise money to fund scientific research.

41. D: It gives the correct defining characteristic of the **Roaring Twenties** Era. The economy was strong with a great demand for new products, while culture in this era, also known as the "Jazz Age," became more experimental. A student might pick choice A, which defines the Cold War Era, if he or she focuses on the fact that it is also an era immediately following a World War. A student can rule out the other choices if they know how to correctly define the World War II and Great Depression Eras.

42. C: Jonathan Trumbull is the correct answer for which Founding Father was governor of Connecticut during and after the Revolutionary War. The other names are all of Founding Fathers, but none were governor of Connecticut. Rush, Witherspoon and Carroll all signed the Declaration of Independence; Carroll was a U.S. Senator for Maryland while Rush lived in Pennsylvania and Witherspoon in New Jersey.

43. A: It shows the student's knowledge of the importance of 1914 events as a turning point for the start of World War I in Europe: "World War I had started; Germany had invaded other Belgian cities and was going to invade Antwerp also." The other choices are incorrect because Italy, Russia, and England were not invading Belgium.

44. D: It lists true contributions by John Jay to early. Choice A is partly correct about the first Chief Justice, but Jay was a Minister to Spain, not to France. Choice B correctly places him in

New York, but he did not sign the Declaration or become mayor of New York City. Choice C has Minister of Spain correct, but Jay did not serve in George Washington's army during the war.

45. D: While the photo shows World War I airplane warfare over England, it also took place over other countries like Germany and France, so choice A is incorrect. Airplane warfare first took place after the invention of the airplane, so during the Civil War could not be a correct choice. The American allies and the German side went back and forth in terms of airplane technology superiority, so choice B is not correct. Choice D is the MOST likely answer choice. Airplanes had their first warfare use during WWI, at first just for taking spy photographs, but were also used later in the war for firing guns and dropping bombs. The photo illustrates the fact that airplanes were in use during WWI for firing guns and dropping bombs.

46. D: Ella Baker was a civil rights leader but born in 1903. Rosa Parks was part of the 1960s civil rights movement. Sojourner Truth lived near the time of Ida B. Wells, but she had died by 1883. Ida B. Wells is the correct answer, and she was known as a journalist, muckraker, reform leader, and fighter against lynchings.

47. A: Sanford B. Dole was the President of the Republic of Hawaii, and he did argue for annexation of Hawaii by the United States. Students familiar with the time period should know that he was not the President of the United States or the President of the U.S. Senate. The excerpt may help them realize this fact. Also, Hawaii did not become a state officially until the 1950s, so choice B is incorrect.

48. B: The BEST summarizing title for the list is "How the Spanish-American War Helped the U.S. Become a World Power." President Theodore Roosevelt did help the U.S. become a world power, but that was after the events on the list (Spanish-American War events) because he was not president until 1901, after the war of 1898. Isolationism did give way to Imperialism in the 1890s, but it did not lead to or cause imperialism. The War of 1812 is an incorrect answer for students who know their historical dates and war events.

49. D: In point 14 of his 1918 speech Wilson was proposing a League of Nations which would eventually become the United Nations. If the student reads the excerpt carefully, and knows general history about the United Nations, the student will know that having the U.S. involved in such a league would be a contrast to Wilson's pre-War policy of neutrality. The other choices given make references to phrases found in the excerpt, but they are not statements that contrast with a policy of neutrality and are incorrect answer choices.

50. D: It is correct for why the Battle of the Argonne Forest was difficult and important. The illustration gives a clue to the answer because it shows a deep trench (though it also shows a forest, so the student also needs general social studies knowledge). The battle was difficult because the Germans were so entrenched in this forest, having built deep trenches there; and important because it was one of the final battles of the war and helped break through Germany's western front. The deeply forested nature of the area mentioned in choice C was also a difficulty, but that choice is incorrect because it claims the Germans won that battle when they did not. Some German soldiers were taken as prisoners of war during the battle, and there may have been some Allied prisoners, but that was not the purpose of the battle. There was air support provided to the Allies in that battle, so choice A is incorrect.

51. A: The 16th Amendment is the correct answer for which amendment dealt with collecting income taxes to help fund progressive government goals. While all the amendments listed were championed by Progressive Era reformers, and all were around the same time period, the other amendments listed dealt with voting issues or prohibition, not with income taxes.

52. C: It is the BEST and only definition of the initiative process: It allowed citizens to introduce legislation proposals at a local or state level by gathering petitions, and proposals would then be addressed by lawmakers or placed on ballots for a vote. The other answer choices give definitions of "referendum" (choice A), "recall" (choice B), and also describe simply visiting a state legislature to give testimony about an issue (choice D), none of which define the "initiative" process.

53. B: "Nativism," a philosophy of the time period that native-born white Americans were superior to foreign born Americans, helped cause the Emergency Quota Act that limited immigrants in 1921. The other options were all social issues of the same time period, but not the main cause for limiting immigration. The Harlem Renaissance and Women's Suffrage Movement did not have such qualms with immigrants. Prohibition was partly caused by anti-immigrant sentiment such as against Germans after WWI, but Prohibition did not cause the Quota Act as much as Nativism.

54. D: It is the correct answer for this particular group of children, although choices A and B might be good guesses. There were German youth who wanted to avoid serving in Nazi armies, but they did not go into hiding in as great numbers as did Jewish youth trying to escape the Holocaust. There were children who awaited fake passports, but mostly to escape to the U.S. or other safe countries, as Israel was not founded until after World War II. The correct answer is that "They were Jewish and had to be hidden from Nazis in order to survive the Holocaust, the attempted extermination of the Jewish population by Nazi Germany."

55. C: It would BEST go next in the timeline's factual sequence of events because the other choices are not factually correct: thousands of Japanese-American men, women and children are relocated to internment camps. They were not forced to leave the U.S., and they were not forced to move from west coast to east coast (many internment camps were on the west coast). Japanese-American men did eventually start to be drafted for military service during World War II, and many did fight in that war for the U.S.

56. C: The clue in the excerpt about American troops helping the stressed French and British troops should let the student know that the excerpt refers to World War I or World War II. If they read closely enough to see General Pershing's involvement, then they should know from general social studies knowledge at this grade level that Pershing was the commander of American Expeditionary Forces during World War I, and therefore C is the correct answer.

57. A: W.E.B. DuBois was a famous African American muckraking journalist for the NAACP's magazine in the early 1900s. Booker T. Washington was a contemporary of DuBois, but not a muckraking journalist. Gaines was a former slave who became a Texas State Senator, but Gaines died in 1900 and therefore could not be the correct answer. Marcus Garvey had a writing career advocating civil rights, but in a newspaper he started called *The Negro World*.

58. B: Students who know about the U.S. Office of War Information should know that the purpose was to get out messages that would build morale and raise spirits. They also tried to recruit women for wartime work during WWII. They sometimes used famous stars such as Ethel Merman to further appeal to women. Their purpose was not to sell Broadway or movie tickets, nor was it to encourage women to stay at home.

59. C: The speech is from President Richard M. Nixon, who was about to become, in 1972, the first U.S. president to visit the People's Republic of China. The other presidents listed are good guesses as they are from similar time periods and might have made similar speeches about China and the Soviet Union, but they are incorrect choices.

60. A: The Fall of Saigon happened in April 1975 and marked the end of the Vietnam War and the beginning of Vietnam's reunification under communist rule. A student might pick one of the other events because they were all events that did happen in the course of the Vietnam War, but they happened on earlier dates, not in April 1975, and were not the final event that marked the end of the war or South Vietnam's surrender.

61. C: The 26th Amendment is the youth voting rights amendment allowing 18-year-olds to vote, signed by President Nixon. The Vietnam War gave more urgency to the "old enough to fight, old enough to vote" slogan. The other amendment choices are in similar time frames and close enough to the 26th Amendment to possibly confuse a student who has not fully studied some of the more important amendments such as the 26th.

62. A: It is the BEST title for the list, The Causes of the 1935 Dust Bowl. The lack of ground cover was a cause of the Dust Bowl, but could also be considered a possible effect of dust storms also. But that is the only item on the list that would also be an effect of the Dust Bowl. The Sun Belt also had some years of drought, but the other items would not fit for Sun Belt as much, or for the Rust Belt except for possibly poor agricultural practices.

63. C: It is the BEST summary of the paragraph's main idea for settlers headed to the Great Plains in stage coach wagons: Fording the Platte River was thought to be dangerous, but turned out to mostly be time-consuming and a little inconvenient: time consuming because it "consumed" a whole day and inconvenient in that drivers and wagon boxes got wet. Choice A is incorrect because the wagon in the paragraph did not get caught in quicksand. Choice B is incorrect because it was not a quick and easy fording (it consumed a whole day). Choice D is a correct and true statement, but it has to do with a detail of the trip after the river crossing, and does not deal with the paragraph's main idea of describing the river crossing.

64. A: The most likely conclusion based on the U.S. Census data chart is that rural to urban migration was a probable trend between the years 1890 and 1930. Both rural and urban areas grew in population numbers, making choices C and D incorrect, but urban areas grew by a much larger margin, meaning that there was probably migration from rural areas in addition to general population growth as a factor for the different numbers. Choice B is incorrect because urban to rural migration numbers are not shown on the chart.

65. C: President Roosevelt's plan for the judicial branch in 1937 was to raise the total number of Supreme Court justices from 9 to 15. His plan was defeated by the U.S. Senate. The other answer choices sound like plausible ways that one might try to "pack the courts,"

but they are not correct answers for that time period, which students with a general history knowledge at this grade level should know.

66. D: Choice A is incorrect because Al Gore was not yet speaking on global warming issues during that time period. Choice B does not make sense in the context of the timeline because all the other events listed deal with environmental issues. Choice C confuses the establishment of the National Park System with the EPA. The park system was established earlier by Theodore Roosevelt, which should be part of the student's general social studies knowledge. Choice D is correct: Nixon established the EPA in December 1970.

67. D: Student sit-ins were an example in the 1960s of non-violent protesting that took place mostly under the guidance and philosophy of Martin Luther King, Jr. These were not displays of Black Power to incite fear, although those also occurred separately in the 1960s under leaders such as Malcolm X. Sit-ins were not a form of lobbying or litigation, although those are also non-violent in their nature.

68. A: It is the best conclusion to be made based on the facts in the excerpt: Jobs for African Americans increased during World War II because of manpower needs and because of an anti-discrimination order from the president. The jobs would not have come without the executive order because there was still a lot of discrimination against African Americans in the 1940s (as is described in Coombs' book, paragraphs just before and after this excerpt). Roosevelt was concerned about Randolph planning a march because of how it might appear to U.S. enemies during the war, and Randolph was not bluffing. Randolph said discrimination by whites, not his march, was the reason that the U.S. would appear in a poor light to enemies or other countries.

69. B: The G.I. Bill, or Servicemen's Readjustment Act of 1944, was the name of the bill that had the myriad effects listed in the chart. The Taft-Hartley Act was an anti-labor bill under Truman; the Smith Act was a war time bill under FDR in 1940; and the Executive Order listed was one signed by Truman (although it would be a good guess because FDR did sign many "Executive Orders"). All the distracters are also near the same time period as the GI Bill, but students with a good general knowledge of history should get the correct answer.

70. A: Increased consumer spending and consumption can BEST be linked to the other three trends of the 1950s. An argument could be made that rock and roll music was also an effect, but that cannot be tied directly to other three factors listed in the question, and it is a more specific and less general answer and therefore less correct answer for being in a cause/effect relationship with the other general trends. The military-industrial complex and Cold War were other trends in the 1950s, but they were not tied to the three trends mentioned in the question.

71. D: Federalists who helped frame the Constitution believed the central government needed to be stronger than what was established under the Articles of Confederation. Anti-federalists were against this and feared a strong federal government. A system of checks and balances was established to prevent the central government from taking too much power.

72. A: The Senate and House of Representatives make up a bicameral legislature. The Great Compromise awarded seats in the Senate equally to each state, while the seats in the House of Representatives were based on population.

73. C: The Civil Rights Act of 1964 affected the Jim Crowe laws in the Southern states. Many minorities suffered under unfair voting laws and segregation. President Lyndon Johnson signed the Civil Rights Act of 1964 into law after the 1963 assassination of President Kennedy, who championed the reform.

74. B: President John Adams appointed William Marbury as Justice of the Peace, but Secretary of State James Madison never delivered the commission. Marbury claimed that under the Judiciary Act of 1789, the Supreme Court could order his commission be given to him. The Supreme Court denied Marbury's petition citing that the Judiciary Act of 1789 was unconstitutional, although they believed he was entitled to his commission.

75. D: The Bill of Rights was drafted by Congress to limit the authority of the government and protect the rights of individual citizens from abuse by the federal government. It was the first document to detail the rights of private citizens.

76. B: The Supreme Court ruled that statements made in interrogation are not admissible unless the defendant is informed of the right to an attorney and waives that right. The case of Miranda v. Arizona was consolidated with Westover v. United States, Vignera v. New York, and California v. Stewart.

77. D: America is a common law country because English common law was adopted in all states except Louisiana. Common law is based on precedent, and changes over time. Each state develops its own common laws.

78. A: James Madison, John Jay, and Alexander Hamilton published The Federalist in the Independent Journal in New York. It was a response to the Anti-Federalists in New York, who were slow to ratify the Constitution because they feared it gave the central government too much authority.

79. C: The President must be a natural citizen, be at least 35 years old, and have lived in the U.S. for 14 years. There is no education requirement for becoming President. Truman did not have a college education, but most Presidents have degrees.

80. B: Most Presidents have only served two terms, a precedent established by George Washington. Ulysses S. Grant and Theodore Roosevelt sought third terms; however, only Franklin D. Roosevelt served more than two terms. He served a third term and won a fourth, but died in its first year. The 22nd Amendment was passed by Congress in 1947 and ratified in 1951. It officially limited the President to two terms, and a Vice President who serves two years as President only can be elected for one term.

81. C: The 17th Amendment was ratified in 1913. This amendment allowed the citizens to choose their Senators by holding elections and participating in a popular vote.

82. A: Anyone may write a bill, but only a member of Congress can introduce a bill. The President often suggests bills. Bills can change drastically throughout the review process.

83. B: Members of the House are elected for two-year terms. Senators serve six-year terms, but the elections are staggered so roughly one-third of the Senate is elected every two years.

84. D: The Vice President also serves as the President of the Senate. If a tie occurs in the Senate, the Vice President casts his vote to break the tie.

85. C: A bill is usually first reviewed by the appropriate subcommittee. The subcommittee can accept the bill, amend the bill, or reject the bill. If the subcommittee accepts or amends the bill, they send it to the full committee for review. Expert witnesses and testimony are all part of committee review.

86. B: All states have bicameral legislatures, except Nebraska. The bicameral legislatures in states resemble the federal legislature, with an upper house and a lower house.

87. A: The 10th Amendment establishes that any power not given to the federal government in the Constitution belongs to the states, or the people. The federal and local governments share many responsibilities.

88. D: Local governments are usually divided into counties and municipalities. Municipalities oversee parks and recreation services, police and fire departments, housing services, emergency medical services, municipal courts, transportation services, and public works.

89. B: Congress normally chooses the jurisdiction of federal courts. The Supreme Court has original jurisdiction in certain cases, which Congress cannot revoke. For example, the Supreme Court has the right to settle a dispute between states.

90. A: The Supreme Court interprets law and the Constitution. The inferior courts are bound to uphold the law as the Supreme Court interprets and rules on it.

91. C: Informal qualifications are the public's expectations of Presidential candidates. These can vary, but the President is considered by many to be a moral leader. This means the public expects the President to have a strong character, so a criminal record or lapses in moral judgment can prevent a person from becoming President.

92. A: If there is a tie in the Electoral College, each state's delegation in the House of Representatives gets a vote, and the majority wins. The Senate votes on the Vice President who becomes acting President if the House does not come to a conclusion by Inauguration Day. It is possible for the Senate to tie because the former Vice President is not allowed to vote.

93. D: The Senate approves Presidential appointments and treaties. The House must also approve appointments of the Vice Presidency and any treaty involving foreign trade.

94. B: The versions of a bill that pass through both houses of Congress and are signed by the President must have the exact same wording. A conference committee brings the versions of the bill into alignment, but exact wording is rare.

95. C: There are 538 electors in the Electoral College, assigned by population. There is one for each member of the congressional delegation. The District of Columbia has three electors in the Electoral College.

96. D: Public policy covers numerous areas, and special interest groups are often associated with areas of public policy. These interest groups publish their research to influence the public policies that are chosen, such as disabilities, health, education, or human rights.

97. B: A bicameral legislature has more than one legislative house, such as an upper house and a lower house. This form of mixed government is supposed to ensure greater representation since it takes both houses to pass legislation. Many authoritarian or communist regimes have unicameral legislature, or one legislative house. Unicameral legislatures do not ensure equal representation, but they pass legislation faster than bicameral legislatures.

98. A: Nationalism legitimizes authority and establishes unity. Nationalism or secular nationalism influences world views and seeks to manage chaos. Secular nationalism has influenced the founding and formation of different governments throughout history.

99. C: A pluralist society is made up of many distinct special interest groups that represent different social minorities. These interest groups compete with each other to influence legislation. The power special interest groups exert is constantly shifting.

100. B: Most political theorists support free international trade. For example, many liberals, Marxists, social democrats, and conservatives support the idea of free international trade; however, most communist regimes have strict trade limitations.

101. C: Banks create money by giving out loans. For example, assume a person puts $100 into a bank. The bank will keep a percentage of that money in reserves because of the reserve requirement. If the reserve requirement is 10% then the bank will put $10 in reserves and then loan out $90 of it to a second person. The money total, which started at $100, now includes the original $100 plus the $90, or a total of $190. The bank creates $90 by loaning it.

102. D: A supply shock is caused when there is a dramatic increase in input prices. This causes an increase in price levels and decreases in employment and GDP. A supply shock causes the AS curve to move to the left (in).

103. A: The equation of exchange is MV = PQ. This means that M1 (a measure of the supply of money) multiplied by the velocity of money (the average number of times a typical dollar is spent on final goods and services a year) = the average price level of final goods and services in GDP x real output, or the quantity of goods and services in GDP.

104. B: John Maynard Keynes argued that government could help revitalize a recessionary economy by increasing government spending and therefore increasing aggregate demand. This is known as demand-side economics.

105. C: In the short-run Phillips curve, there is a trade-off between unemployment and inflation. There is no such trade-off in the long-run Phillips curve. According to the long-run Phillips curve, the economy tends to stay at the natural rate of unemployment, and any changes are minor variations that will self-correct.

106. C: A person who has taken out a fixed-rate loan can benefit from inflation by paying back the loan with dollars that are less valuable than they were when the loan was taken out. In the other examples, inflation harms the individual or entity.

107. B: When AD for the goods produced by an industry decreases, one might expect the wages paid to workers in that industry to decrease as a result. However, because unions negotiate contracts with employers, wages of unionized workers tend not to fall in these circumstances. This tendency to for wages to stay the same is known as "sticky wages."

108. D: Because the MPC is 0.9, the multiplier is 10 (1/0.1). Therefore, to attain an increase of $10 billion in AD, the government must increase spending by $1 billion ($1 billion x 10 = $10 billion).

109. B: The current account is a measurement of a country's net exports. If a country has a current account surplus, the value of the goods and services it is exporting is greater than the value of the goods and services it is importing.

110. C: The increased cost of gasoline increases the cost of transportation. This is a variable cost of supply, and so the AS curve shifts inward and upward. In the short run, AD would remain fixed, leading to a rise in prices and decreased GDP.

111. E: An increase in the supply of the hats and a decrease in demand would both cause the equilibrium price to decrease, not increase. If both supply and demand stayed the same, the equilibrium price would also stay the same. If government subsidies made it cheaper to produce the hats, the price would go down. If the supply of a substitute good went down, more consumers might be driven to buy the blue hats, causing demand to increase and the equilibrium price to increase with it.

112. C: The law of diminishing marginal utility states that at some point a consumer will notice less satisfaction from a good or service at each consecutive consumption level of that product.

113. A: The accounting profit equals revenues minus costs. Economic profit is also concerned with opportunity costs.

114. C: Because the PPF shows all the combinations of goods that can be produced with a given set of resources, it is bowed, signifying that some combinations of the two goods have different opportunity costs.

115. C: A labor union reduces the supply of labor, thereby raising the wage rate above the equilibrium wage rate that would be earned in a perfectly competitive labor market. The supply curve for labor shifts to the left when a labor market is unionized.

116. D: In the short run, Bob's should continue to operate even if total revenues are less than total costs provide total revenues are at least greater than total variable costs. This means that the variable costs of operating would be covered and at least some of the fixed costs would be covered. In Bob's case, however, total variable

costs are not covered, and so Bob's should shut down instead of incurring greater expenses by continuing to operate.

117. D: By definition, a public good is one that is non-excludable and non-rivalrous. The non-excludable nature of a public good is stated by option D.

118. C: The firms in an oligopoly may collude intentionally or unintentionally. The rest of the options are wrong: an oligopoly has many barriers to entry, including great economies of scale. This creates a "kinked" demand curve. Because of the barriers to entry, an oligopoly has few firms, not many.

119. E: By definition, production in the short run is the time period during which a plant cannot increase production capacity, and production in the long run is the time period during which production capacity can be changed.

120. D: An economic system must decide what goods and services are produced, how they are produced, and who gets them. The economic system will not set supply or demand.

Secret Key #1 - Time is Your Greatest Enemy

Pace Yourself

Wear a watch. At the beginning of the test, check the time (or start a chronometer on your watch to count the minutes), and check the time after every few questions to make sure you are "on schedule."

If you are forced to speed up, do it efficiently. Usually one or more answer choices can be eliminated without too much difficulty. Above all, don't panic. Don't speed up and just begin guessing at random choices. By pacing yourself, and continually monitoring your progress against your watch, you will always know exactly how far ahead or behind you are with your available time. If you find that you are one minute behind on the test, don't skip one question without spending any time on it, just to catch back up. Take 15 fewer seconds on the next four questions, and after four questions you'll have caught back up. Once you catch back up, you can continue working each problem at your normal pace.

Furthermore, don't dwell on the problems that you were rushed on. If a problem was taking up too much time and you made a hurried guess, it must be difficult. The difficult questions are the ones you are most likely to miss anyway, so it isn't a big loss. It is better to end with more time than you need than to run out of time.

Lastly, sometimes it is beneficial to slow down if you are constantly getting ahead of time. You are always more likely to catch a careless mistake by working more slowly than quickly, and among very high-scoring test takers (those who are likely to have lots of time left over), careless errors affect the score more than mastery of material.

Secret Key #2 - Guessing is not Guesswork

You probably know that guessing is a good idea. Unlike other standardized tests, there is no penalty for getting a wrong answer. Even if you have no idea about a question, you still have a 20-25% chance of getting it right.

Most test takers do not understand the impact that proper guessing can have on their score. Unless you score extremely high, guessing will significantly contribute to your final score.

Monkeys Take the Test

What most test takers don't realize is that to insure that 20-25% chance, you have to guess randomly. If you put 20 monkeys in a room to take this test, assuming they answered once per question and behaved themselves, on average they would get 20-25% of the questions correct. Put 20 test takers in the room, and the average will be much lower among guessed questions. Why?
1. The test writers intentionally write deceptive answer choices that "look" right. A test taker has no idea about a question, so he picks the "best looking" answer, which is often wrong. The monkey has no idea what looks good and what doesn't, so it will consistently be right about 20-25% of the time.
2. Test takers will eliminate answer choices from the guessing pool based on a hunch or intuition. Simple but correct answers often get excluded, leaving a 0% chance of being correct. The monkey has no clue, and often gets lucky with the best choice.

This is why the process of elimination endorsed by most test courses is flawed and detrimental to your performance. Test takers don't guess; they make an ignorant stab in the dark that is usually worse than random.

$5 Challenge

Let me introduce one of the most valuable ideas of this course—the $5 challenge:

You only mark your "best guess" if you are willing to bet $5 on it.
You only eliminate choices from guessing if you are willing to bet $5 on it.

Why $5? Five dollars is an amount of money that is small yet not insignificant, and can really add up fast (20 questions could cost you $100). Likewise, each answer choice on one question of the test will have a small impact on your overall score, but it can really add up to a lot of points in the end.

The process of elimination IS valuable. The following shows your chance of guessing it right:

If you eliminate wrong answer choices until only this many remain:	Chance of getting it correct:
1	100%
2	50%
3	33%

However, if you accidentally eliminate the right answer or go on a hunch for an incorrect answer, your chances drop dramatically—to 0%. By guessing among all the answer choices, you are GUARANTEED to have a shot at the right answer.

That's why the $5 test is so valuable. If you give up the advantage and safety of a pure guess, it had better be worth the risk.

What we still haven't covered is how to be sure that whatever guess you make is truly random. Here's the easiest way:

Always pick the first answer choice among those remaining.

Such a technique means that you have decided, **before you see a single test question**, exactly how you are going to guess, and since the order of choices tells you nothing about which one is correct, this guessing technique is perfectly random.

This section is not meant to scare you away from making educated guesses or eliminating choices; you just need to define when a choice is worth eliminating. The $5 test, along with a pre-defined random guessing strategy, is the best way to make sure you reap all of the benefits of guessing.

Secret Key #3 - Practice Smarter, Not Harder

Many test takers delay the test preparation process because they dread the awful amounts of practice time they think necessary to succeed on the test. We have refined an effective method that will take you only a fraction of the time.

There are a number of "obstacles" in the path to success. Among these are answering questions, finishing in time, and mastering test-taking strategies. All must be executed on the day of the test at peak performance, or your score will suffer. The test is a mental marathon that has a large impact on your future.

Just like a marathon runner, it is important to work your way up to the full challenge. So first you just worry about questions, and then time, and finally strategy:

Success Strategy

1. Find a good source for practice tests.
2. If you are willing to make a larger time investment, consider using more than one study guide. Often the different approaches of multiple authors will help you "get" difficult concepts.
3. Take a practice test with no time constraints, with all study helps, "open book." Take your time with questions and focus on applying strategies.
4. Take a practice test with time constraints, with all guides, "open book."
5. Take a final practice test without open material and with time limits.

If you have time to take more practice tests, just repeat step 5. By gradually exposing yourself to the full rigors of the test environment, you will condition your mind to the stress of test day and maximize your success.

Secret Key #4 - Prepare, Don't Procrastinate

Let me state an obvious fact: if you take the test three times, you will probably get three different scores. This is due to the way you feel on test day, the level of preparedness you have, and the version of the test you see. Despite the test writers' claims to the contrary, some versions of the test WILL be easier for you than others.

Since your future depends so much on your score, you should maximize your chances of success. In order to maximize the likelihood of success, you've got to prepare in advance. This means taking practice tests and spending time learning the information and test taking strategies you will need to succeed.

Never go take the actual test as a "practice" test, expecting that you can just take it again if you need to. Take all the practice tests you can on your own, but when you go to take the official test, be prepared, be focused, and do your best the first time!

Secret Key #5 - Test Yourself

Everyone knows that time is money. There is no need to spend too much of your time or too little of your time preparing for the test. You should only spend as much of your precious time preparing as is necessary for you to get the score you need.

Once you have taken a practice test under real conditions of time constraints, then you will know if you are ready for the test or not.

If you have scored extremely high the first time that you take the practice test, then there is not much point in spending countless hours studying. You are already there.

Benchmark your abilities by retaking practice tests and seeing how much you have improved. Once you consistently score high enough to guarantee success, then you are ready.

If you have scored well below where you need, then knuckle down and begin studying in earnest. Check your improvement regularly through the use of practice tests under real conditions. Above all, don't worry, panic, or give up. The key is perseverance!

Then, when you go to take the test, remain confident and remember how well you did on the practice tests. If you can score high enough on a practice test, then you can do the same on the real thing.

General Strategies

The most important thing you can do is to ignore your fears and jump into the test immediately. Do not be overwhelmed by any strange-sounding terms. You have to jump into the test like jumping into a pool—all at once is the easiest way.

Make Predictions

As you read and understand the question, try to guess what the answer will be. Remember that several of the answer choices are wrong, and once you begin reading them, your mind will immediately become cluttered with answer choices designed to throw you off. Your mind is typically the most focused immediately after you have read the question and digested its contents. If you can, try to predict what the correct answer will be. You may be surprised at what you can predict.

Quickly scan the choices and see if your prediction is in the listed answer choices. If it is, then you can be quite confident that you have the right answer. It still won't hurt to check the other answer choices, but most of the time, you've got it!

Answer the Question

It may seem obvious to only pick answer choices that answer the question, but the test writers can create some excellent answer choices that are wrong. Don't pick an answer just because it sounds right, or you believe it to be true. It MUST answer the question. Once you've made your selection, always go back and check it against the question and make sure that you didn't misread the question and that the answer choice does answer the question posed.

Benchmark

After you read the first answer choice, decide if you think it sounds correct or not. If it doesn't, move on to the next answer choice. If it does, mentally mark that answer choice. This doesn't mean that you've definitely selected it as your answer choice, it just means that it's the best you've seen thus far. Go ahead and read the next choice. If the next choice is worse than the one you've already selected, keep going to the next answer choice. If the next choice is better than the choice you've already selected, mentally mark the new answer choice as your best guess.

The first answer choice that you select becomes your standard. Every other answer choice must be benchmarked against that standard. That choice is correct until proven otherwise by another answer choice beating it out. Once you've decided that no other answer choice seems as good, do one final check to ensure that your answer choice answers the question posed.

Valid Information

Don't discount any of the information provided in the question. Every piece of information may be necessary to determine the correct answer. None of the information in the question is there to throw you off (while the answer choices will certainly have information to throw you off). If two seemingly unrelated topics are discussed, don't ignore either. You can be confident there is a relationship, or it wouldn't be included in the question, and you are probably going to have to determine what is that relationship to find the answer.

Avoid "Fact Traps"

Don't get distracted by a choice that is factually true. Your search is for the answer that answers the question. Stay focused and don't fall for an answer that is true but irrelevant. Always go back to the question and make sure you're choosing an answer that actually answers the question and is not just a true statement. An answer can be factually correct, but it MUST answer the question asked. Additionally, two answers can both be seemingly correct, so be sure to read all of the answer choices, and make sure that you get the one that BEST answers the question.

Milk the Question

Some of the questions may throw you completely off. They might deal with a subject you have not been exposed to, or one that you haven't reviewed in years. While your lack of knowledge about the subject will be a hindrance, the question itself can give you many clues that will help you find the correct answer. Read the question carefully and look for clues. Watch particularly for adjectives and nouns describing difficult terms or words that you don't recognize. Regardless of whether you completely understand a word or not, replacing it with a synonym, either provided or one you more familiar with, may help you to understand what the questions are asking. Rather than wracking your mind about specific detailed information concerning a difficult term or word, try to use mental substitutes that are easier to understand.

The Trap of Familiarity

Don't just choose a word because you recognize it. On difficult questions, you may not recognize a number of words in the answer choices. The test writers don't put "make-believe" words on the test, so don't think that just because you only recognize all the words in one answer choice that that answer choice must be correct. If you only recognize words in one answer choice, then focus on that one. Is it correct? Try your best to determine if it is correct. If it is, that's great. If not, eliminate it. Each word and answer choice you eliminate increases your chances of getting the question correct, even if you then have to guess among the unfamiliar choices.

Eliminate Answers

Eliminate choices as soon as you realize they are wrong. But be careful! Make sure you consider all of the possible answer choices. Just because one appears right, doesn't mean that the next one won't be even better! The test writers will usually put more than one good answer choice for every question, so read all of them. Don't worry if you are stuck between two that seem right. By getting down to just two remaining possible choices, your odds are now 50/50. Rather than wasting too much time, play the odds. You are guessing, but guessing wisely because you've been able to knock out some of the answer choices that you know are wrong. If you are eliminating choices and realize that the last answer choice you are left with is also obviously wrong, don't panic. Start over and consider each choice again. There may easily be something that you missed the first time and will realize on the second pass.

Tough Questions

If you are stumped on a problem or it appears too hard or too difficult, don't waste time. Move on! Remember though, if you can quickly check for obviously incorrect answer choices, your chances of guessing correctly are greatly improved. Before you completely give up, at least try to knock out a couple of possible answers. Eliminate what you can and then guess at the remaining answer choices before moving on.

Brainstorm

If you get stuck on a difficult question, spend a few seconds quickly brainstorming. Run through the complete list of possible answer choices. Look at each choice and ask yourself, "Could this answer the question satisfactorily?" Go through each answer choice and consider it independently of the others. By systematically going through all possibilities, you may find something that you would otherwise overlook. Remember though that when you get stuck, it's important to try to keep moving.

Read Carefully

Understand the problem. Read the question and answer choices carefully. Don't miss the question because you misread the terms. You have plenty of time to read each question thoroughly and make sure you understand what is being asked. Yet a happy medium must be attained, so don't waste too much time. You must read carefully, but efficiently.

Face Value

When in doubt, use common sense. Always accept the situation in the problem at face value. Don't read too much into it. These problems will not require you to make huge leaps of logic. The test writers aren't trying to throw you off with a cheap trick. If you have to go beyond creativity and make a leap of logic in order to have an answer choice answer the question, then you should look at the other answer choices. Don't overcomplicate the problem by creating theoretical relationships or explanations that will warp time or space. These are normal problems rooted in reality. It's just that the applicable relationship or explanation may not be readily apparent and you have to figure things out. Use your common sense to interpret anything that isn't clear.

Prefixes

If you're having trouble with a word in the question or answer choices, try dissecting it. Take advantage of every clue that the word might include. Prefixes and suffixes can be a huge help. Usually they allow you to determine a basic meaning. Pre- means before, post- means after, pro - is positive, de- is negative. From these prefixes and suffixes, you can get an idea of the general meaning of the word and try to put it into context. Beware though of any traps. Just because con- is the opposite of pro-, doesn't necessarily mean congress is the opposite of progress!

Hedge Phrases

Watch out for critical hedge phrases, led off with words such as "likely," "may," "can," "sometimes," "often," "almost," "mostly," "usually," "generally," "rarely," and "sometimes." Question writers insert these hedge phrases to cover every possibility. Often an answer choice will be wrong simply because it leaves no room for exception. Unless the situation calls for them, avoid answer choices that have definitive words like "exactly," and "always."

Switchback Words

Stay alert for "switchbacks." These are the words and phrases frequently used to alert you to shifts in thought. The most common switchback word is "but." Others include "although," "however," "nevertheless," "on the other hand," "even though," "while," "in spite of," "despite," and "regardless of."

New Information

Correct answer choices will rarely have completely new information included. Answer choices typically are straightforward reflections of the material asked about and will directly relate to the question. If a new piece of information is included in an answer choice that doesn't even seem to relate to the topic being asked about, then that answer choice is likely incorrect. All of the information needed to answer the question is usually provided for you in the question. You should not have to make guesses that are unsupported or choose answer choices that require unknown information that cannot be reasoned from what is given.

Time Management

On technical questions, don't get lost on the technical terms. Don't spend too much time on any one question. If you don't know what a term means, then odds are you aren't going to get much further since you don't have a dictionary. You should be able to immediately recognize whether or not you know a term. If you don't, work with the other clues that you have—the other answer choices and terms provided—but don't waste too much time trying to figure out a difficult term that you don't know.

Contextual Clues

Look for contextual clues. An answer can be right but not the correct answer. The contextual clues will help you find the answer that is most right and is correct. Understand the context in which a phrase or statement is made. This will help you make important distinctions.

Don't Panic

Panicking will not answer any questions for you; therefore, it isn't helpful. When you first see the question, if your mind goes blank, take a deep breath. Force yourself to mechanically go through the steps of solving the problem using the strategies you've learned.

Pace Yourself

Don't get clock fever. It's easy to be overwhelmed when you're looking at a page full of questions, your mind is full of random thoughts and feeling confused, and the clock is ticking down faster than you would like. Calm down and maintain the pace that you have set for yourself. As long as you are on track by monitoring your pace, you are guaranteed to have enough time for yourself. When you get to the last few minutes of the test, it may seem like you won't have enough time left, but if you only have as many questions as you should have left at that point, then you're right on track!

Answer Selection

The best way to pick an answer choice is to eliminate all of those that are wrong, until only one is left and confirm that is the correct answer. Sometimes though, an answer choice may immediately look right. Be careful! Take a second to make sure that the other choices are not equally obvious. Don't make a hasty mistake. There are only two times that you should stop before checking other answers. First is when you are positive that the answer choice you have selected is correct. Second is when time is almost out and you have to make a quick guess!

Check Your Work

Since you will probably not know every term listed and the answer to every question, it is important that you get credit for the ones that you do know. Don't miss any questions through careless mistakes. If at all possible, try to take a second to look back over your answer selection and make sure you've selected the correct answer choice and haven't made a costly careless mistake (such as marking an answer choice that you didn't mean to mark). The time it takes for this quick double check should more than pay for itself in caught mistakes.

Beware of Directly Quoted Answers

Sometimes an answer choice will repeat word for word a portion of the question or reference section. However, beware of such exact duplication. It may be a trap! More than likely, the correct choice will paraphrase or summarize a point, rather than being exactly the same wording.

Slang

Scientific sounding answers are better than slang ones. An answer choice that begins "To compare the outcomes..." is much more likely to be correct than one that begins "Because some people insisted..."

Extreme Statements

Avoid wild answers that throw out highly controversial ideas that are proclaimed as established fact. An answer choice that states the "process should used in certain situations, if..." is much more likely to be correct than one that states the "process should be discontinued completely." The first is a calm rational statement and doesn't even make a definitive, uncompromising stance, using a hedge word "if" to provide wiggle room, whereas the second choice is a radical idea and far more extreme.

Answer Choice Families

When you have two or more answer choices that are direct opposites or parallels, one of them is usually the correct answer. For instance, if one answer choice states "x increases" and another answer choice states "x decreases" or "y increases," then those two or three answer choices are very similar in construction and fall into the same family of answer choices. A family of answer choices consists of two or three answer choices, very similar in construction, but often with directly opposite meanings. Usually the correct answer choice will be in that family of answer choices. The "odd man out" or answer choice that doesn't seem to fit the parallel construction of the other answer choices is more likely to be incorrect.

Special Report: How to Overcome Test Anxiety

The very nature of tests caters to some level of anxiety, nervousness, or tension, just as we feel for any important event that occurs in our lives. A little bit of anxiety or nervousness can be a good thing. It helps us with motivation, and makes achievement just that much sweeter. However, too much anxiety can be a problem, especially if it hinders our ability to function and perform.

"Test anxiety," is the term that refers to the emotional reactions that some test-takers experience when faced with a test or exam. Having a fear of testing and exams is based upon a rational fear, since the test-taker's performance can shape the course of an academic career. Nevertheless, experiencing excessive fear of examinations will only interfere with the test-taker's ability to perform and chance to be successful.

There are a large variety of causes that can contribute to the development and sensation of test anxiety. These include, but are not limited to, lack of preparation and worrying about issues surrounding the test.

Lack of Preparation

Lack of preparation can be identified by the following behaviors or situations:

Not scheduling enough time to study, and therefore cramming the night before the test or exam
Managing time poorly, to create the sensation that there is not enough time to do everything
Failing to organize the text information in advance, so that the study material consists of the entire text and not simply the pertinent information
Poor overall studying habits

Worrying, on the other hand, can be related to both the test taker, or many other factors around him/her that will be affected by the results of the test. These include worrying about:

Previous performances on similar exams, or exams in general
How friends and other students are achieving
The negative consequences that will result from a poor grade or failure

There are three primary elements to test anxiety. Physical components, which involve the same typical bodily reactions as those to acute anxiety (to be discussed below). Emotional factors have to do with fear or panic. Mental or cognitive issues concerning attention spans and memory abilities.

Physical Signals

There are many different symptoms of test anxiety, and these are not limited to mental and emotional strain. Frequently there are a range of physical signals that will let a test taker know that he/she is suffering from test anxiety. These bodily changes can include the following:

Perspiring
Sweaty palms
Wet, trembling hands
Nausea
Dry mouth
A knot in the stomach
Headache
Faintness
Muscle tension
Aching shoulders, back and neck
Rapid heart beat
Feeling too hot/cold

To recognize the sensation of test anxiety, a test-taker should monitor him/herself for the following sensations:

The physical distress symptoms as listed above
Emotional sensitivity, expressing emotional feelings such as the need to cry or laugh too much, or a sensation of anger or helplessness
A decreased ability to think, causing the test-taker to blank out or have racing thoughts that are hard to organize or control.

Though most students will feel some level of anxiety when faced with a test or exam, the majority can cope with that anxiety and maintain it at a manageable level. However, those who cannot are faced with a very real and very serious condition, which can and should be controlled for the immeasurable benefit of this sufferer.

Naturally, these sensations lead to negative results for the testing experience. The most common effects of test anxiety have to do with nervousness and mental blocking.

Nervousness

Nervousness can appear in several different levels:

The test-taker's difficulty, or even inability to read and understand the questions on the test
The difficulty or inability to organize thoughts to a coherent form
The difficulty or inability to recall key words and concepts relating to the testing questions (especially essays)
The receipt of poor grades on a test, though the test material was well known by the test taker

Conversely, a person may also experience mental blocking, which involves:

Blanking out on test questions
Only remembering the correct answers to the questions when the test has already finished.

Fortunately for test anxiety sufferers, beating these feelings, to a large degree, has to do with proper preparation. When a test taker has a feeling of preparedness, then anxiety will be dramatically lessened.

The first step to resolving anxiety issues is to distinguish which of the two types of anxiety are being suffered. If the anxiety is a direct result of a lack of preparation, this should be considered a normal reaction, and the anxiety level (as opposed to the test results) shouldn't be anything to worry about. However, if, when adequately prepared, the test-taker still panics, blanks out, or seems to overreact, this is not a fully rational reaction. While this can be considered normal too, there are many ways to combat and overcome these effects.

Remember that anxiety cannot be entirely eliminated, however, there are ways to minimize it, to make the anxiety easier to manage. Preparation is one of the best ways to minimize test anxiety. Therefore the following techniques are wise in order to best fight off any anxiety that may want to build.

To begin with, try to avoid cramming before a test, whenever it is possible. By trying to memorize an entire term's worth of information in one day, you'll be shocking your system, and not giving yourself a very good chance to absorb the information. This is an easy path to anxiety, so for those who suffer from test anxiety, cramming should not even be considered an option.

Instead of cramming, work throughout the semester to combine all of the material which is presented throughout the semester, and work on it gradually as the course goes by, making sure to master the main concepts first, leaving minor details for a week or so before the test.

To study for the upcoming exam, be sure to pose questions that may be on the examination, to gauge the ability to answer them by integrating the ideas from your texts, notes and lectures, as well as any supplementary readings.

If it is truly impossible to cover all of the information that was covered in that particular term, concentrate on the most important portions, that can be covered very well. Learn these concepts as best as possible, so that when the test comes, a goal can be made to use these concepts as presentations of your knowledge.

In addition to study habits, changes in attitude are critical to beating a struggle with test anxiety. In fact, an improvement of the perspective over the entire test-taking experience can actually help a test taker to enjoy studying and therefore improve the overall experience. Be certain not to overemphasize the significance of the grade - know that the result of the test is neither a reflection of self worth, nor is it a measure of intelligence; one grade will not predict a person's future success.

To improve an overall testing outlook, the following steps should be tried:

Keeping in mind that the most reasonable expectation for taking a test is to expect to try to demonstrate as much of what you know as you possibly can.
Reminding ourselves that a test is only one test; this is not the only one, and there will be others.
The thought of thinking of oneself in an irrational, all-or-nothing term should be avoided at all costs.
A reward should be designated for after the test, so there's something to look forward to. Whether it be going to a movie, going out to eat, or simply visiting friends, schedule it in advance, and do it no matter what result is expected on the exam.

Test-takers should also keep in mind that the basics are some of the most important things, even beyond anti-anxiety techniques and studying. Never neglect the basic social, emotional and biological needs, in order to try to absorb information. In order to best achieve, these three factors must be held as just as important as the studying itself.

Study Steps

Remember the following important steps for studying:

Maintain healthy nutrition and exercise habits. Continue both your recreational activities and social pass times. These both contribute to your physical and emotional well being.
Be certain to get a good amount of sleep, especially the night before the test, because when you're overtired you are not able to perform to the best of your best ability.
Keep the studying pace to a moderate level by taking breaks when they are needed, and varying the work whenever possible, to keep the mind fresh instead of getting bored.
When enough studying has been done that all the material that can be learned has been learned, and the test taker is prepared for the test, stop studying and do something relaxing such as listening to music, watching a movie, or taking a warm bubble bath.

There are also many other techniques to minimize the uneasiness or apprehension that is experienced along with test anxiety before, during, or even after the examination. In fact, there are a great deal of things that can be done to stop anxiety from interfering with lifestyle and performance. Again, remember that anxiety will not be eliminated entirely, and it shouldn't be. Otherwise that "up" feeling for exams would not exist, and most of us depend on that sensation to perform better than usual. However, this anxiety has to be at a level that is manageable.

Of course, as we have just discussed, being prepared for the exam is half the battle right away. Attending all classes, finding out what knowledge will be expected on the exam, and knowing the exam schedules are easy steps to lowering anxiety. Keeping up with work will remove the need to cram, and efficient study habits will eliminate wasted time. Studying should be done in an ideal location for concentration, so that it is simple to become interested in the material and give it complete attention. A method such as SQ3R (Survey, Question, Read, Recite, Review) is a wonderful key to follow to make sure that the study habits are as effective as possible, especially in the case of learning from a textbook. Flashcards are great techniques for memorization. Learning to take good notes will mean that notes will be full of useful information, so that less sifting will need to be done to seek out what is pertinent for studying. Reviewing notes after class and then again on occasion will keep the information fresh in the mind. From notes that have been taken summary sheets and outlines can be made for simpler reviewing.

A study group can also be a very motivational and helpful place to study, as there will be a sharing of ideas, all of the minds can work together, to make sure that everyone understands, and the studying will be made more interesting because it will be a social occasion.

Basically, though, as long as the test-taker remains organized and self confident, with efficient study habits, less time will need to be spent studying, and higher grades will be achieved.

To become self confident, there are many useful steps. The first of these is "self talk." It has been shown through extensive research, that self-talk for students who suffer from test anxiety, should be well monitored, in order to make sure that it contributes to self confidence as opposed to sinking the student. Frequently the self talk of test-anxious students is negative or self-defeating, thinking that everyone else is smarter and faster, that they always mess up, and that if they don't do well, they'll fail the entire course. It is important to decreasing anxiety that awareness is made of self talk. Try writing any negative self thoughts and then disputing them with a positive statement instead. Begin self-encouragement as though it was a friend speaking. Repeat positive statements to help reprogram the mind to believing in successes instead of failures.

Helpful Techniques

Other extremely helpful techniques include:

Self-visualization of doing well and reaching goals
While aiming for an "A" level of understanding, don't try to "overprotect" by setting your expectations lower. This will only convince the mind to stop studying in order to meet the lower expectations.
Don't make comparisons with the results or habits of other students. These are individual factors, and different things work for different people, causing different results.
Strive to become an expert in learning what works well, and what can be done in order to improve. Consider collecting this data in a journal.
Create rewards for after studying instead of doing things before studying that will only turn into avoidance behaviors.
Make a practice of relaxing - by using methods such as progressive relaxation, self-hypnosis, guided imagery, etc - in order to make relaxation an automatic sensation.
Work on creating a state of relaxed concentration so that concentrating will take on the focus of the mind, so that none will be wasted on worrying.
Take good care of the physical self by eating well and getting enough sleep.
Plan in time for exercise and stick to this plan.

Beyond these techniques, there are other methods to be used before, during and after the test that will help the test-taker perform well in addition to overcoming anxiety.

Before the exam comes the academic preparation. This involves establishing a study schedule and beginning at least one week before the actual date of the test. By doing this, the anxiety of not having enough time to study for the test will be automatically eliminated. Moreover, this will make the studying a much more effective experience, ensuring that the learning will be an easier process. This relieves much undue pressure on the test-taker.

Summary sheets, note cards, and flash cards with the main concepts and examples of these main concepts should be prepared in advance of the actual studying time. A topic should never be eliminated from this process. By omitting a topic because it isn't expected to be on the test is only setting up the test-taker for anxiety should it actually appear on the exam. Utilize the course syllabus for laying out the topics that should be studied. Carefully go over the notes that were made in class, paying special attention to any of the issues that the professor took special care to emphasize while lecturing in class. In the textbooks, use the chapter review, or if possible, the chapter tests, to begin your review.

It may even be possible to ask the instructor what information will be covered on the exam, or what the format of the exam will be (for example, multiple choice, essay, free form, true-false). Additionally, see if it is possible to find out how many questions will be on the test. If a review sheet or sample test has been offered by the professor, make good use of it, above anything else, for the preparation for the test. Another great resource for getting to know the examination is reviewing tests from previous semesters. Use these tests to review, and aim to achieve a 100% score on each of the possible topics. With a few exceptions, the goal that you set for yourself is the highest one that you will reach.

Take all of the questions that were assigned as homework, and rework them to any other possible course material. The more problems reworked, the more skill and confidence will form as a result. When forming the solution to a problem, write out each of the steps. Don't simply do head work. By doing as many steps on paper as possible, much clarification and therefore confidence will be formed. Do this with as many homework problems as possible, before checking the answers. By checking the answer after each problem, a reinforcement will exist, that will not be on the exam. Study situations should be as exam-like as possible, to prime the test-taker's system for the experience. By waiting to check the answers at the end, a psychological advantage will be formed, to decrease the stress factor.

Another fantastic reason for not cramming is the avoidance of confusion in concepts, especially when it comes to mathematics. 8-10 hours of study will become one hundred percent more effective if it is spread out over a week or at least several days, instead of doing it all in one sitting. Recognize that the human brain requires time in order to assimilate new material, so frequent breaks and a span of study time over several days will be much more beneficial.

Additionally, don't study right up until the point of the exam. Studying should stop a minimum of one hour before the exam begins. This allows the brain to rest and put things in their proper order. This will also provide the time to become as relaxed as possible when going into the examination room. The test-taker will also have time to eat well and eat sensibly. Know that the brain needs food as much as the rest of the body. With enough food and enough sleep, as well as a relaxed attitude, the body and the mind are primed for success.

Avoid any anxious classmates who are talking about the exam. These students only spread anxiety, and are not worth sharing the anxious sentimentalities.

Before the test also involves creating a positive attitude, so mental preparation should also be a point of concentration. There are many keys to creating a positive attitude. Should fears become rushing in, make a visualization of taking the exam, doing well, and seeing an A written on the paper. Write out a list of affirmations that will bring a feeling of confidence, such as "I am doing well in my English class," "I studied well and know my material," "I enjoy this class." Even if the affirmations aren't believed at first, it sends a positive message to the subconscious which will result in an alteration of the overall belief system, which is the system that creates reality.

If a sensation of panic begins, work with the fear and imagine the very worst! Work through the entire scenario of not passing the test, failing the entire course, and dropping out of school, followed by not getting a job, and pushing a shopping cart through the dark alley where you'll live. This will place things into perspective! Then, practice deep breathing and create a visualization of the opposite situation - achieving an "A" on the exam, passing the entire course, receiving the degree at a graduation ceremony.

On the day of the test, there are many things to be done to ensure the best results, as well as the most calm outlook. The following stages are suggested in order to maximize test-taking potential:

Begin the examination day with a moderate breakfast, and avoid any coffee or beverages with caffeine if the test taker is prone to jitters. Even people who are used to managing caffeine can feel jittery or light-headed when it is taken on a test day. Attempt to do something that is relaxing before the examination begins. As last minute cramming clouds the mastering of overall concepts, it is better to use this time to create a calming outlook.
Be certain to arrive at the test location well in advance, in order to provide time to select a location that is away from doors, windows and other distractions, as well as giving enough time to relax before the test begins.
Keep away from anxiety generating classmates who will upset the sensation of stability and relaxation that is being attempted before the exam.
Should the waiting period before the exam begins cause anxiety, create a self-distraction by reading a light magazine or something else that is relaxing and simple.

During the exam itself, read the entire exam from beginning to end, and find out how much time should be allotted to each individual problem. Once writing the exam, should more time be taken for a problem, it should be abandoned, in order to begin another problem. If there is time at the end, the unfinished problem can always be returned to and completed.

Read the instructions very carefully - twice - so that unpleasant surprises won't follow during or after the exam has ended.

When writing the exam, pretend that the situation is actually simply the completion of homework within a library, or at home. This will assist in forming a relaxed atmosphere, and will allow the brain extra focus for the complex thinking function.

Begin the exam with all of the questions with which the most confidence is felt. This will build the confidence level regarding the entire exam and will begin a quality momentum. This will also create encouragement for trying the problems where uncertainty resides.

Going with the "gut instinct" is always the way to go when solving a problem. Second guessing should be avoided at all costs. Have confidence in the ability to do well.

For essay questions, create an outline in advance that will keep the mind organized and make certain that all of the points are remembered. For multiple choice, read every answer, even if the correct one has been spotted - a better one may exist.

Continue at a pace that is reasonable and not rushed, in order to be able to work carefully. Provide enough time to go over the answers at the end, to check for small errors that can be corrected.

Should a feeling of panic begin, breathe deeply, and think of the feeling of the body releasing sand through its pores. Visualize a calm, peaceful place, and include all of the sights, sounds and sensations of this image. Continue the deep breathing, and take a few minutes to continue this with closed eyes. When all is well again, return to the test.

If a "blanking" occurs for a certain question, skip it and move on to the next question. There will be time to return to the other question later. Get everything done that can be done, first, to guarantee all the grades that can be compiled, and to build all of the confidence possible. Then return to the weaker questions to build the marks from there.

Remember, one's own reality can be created, so as long as the belief is there, success will follow. And remember: anxiety can happen later, right now, there's an exam to be written!

After the examination is complete, whether there is a feeling for a good grade or a bad grade, don't dwell on the exam, and be certain to follow through on the reward that was promised...and enjoy it! Don't dwell on any mistakes that have been made, as there is nothing that can be done at this point anyway.

Additionally, don't begin to study for the next test right away. Do something relaxing for a while, and let the mind relax and prepare itself to begin absorbing information again.

From the results of the exam - both the grade and the entire experience, be certain to learn from what has gone on. Perfect studying habits and work some more on confidence in order to make the next examination experience even better than the last one.

Learn to avoid places where openings occurred for laziness, procrastination and day dreaming.

Use the time between this exam and the next one to better learn to relax, even learning to relax on cue, so that any anxiety can be controlled during the next exam. Learn how to relax the body. Slouch in your chair if that helps. Tighten and then relax all of the different muscle groups, one group at a time, beginning with the feet and then working all the way up to the neck and face. This will ultimately relax the muscles more than they were to begin with. Learn how to breathe deeply and comfortably, and focus on this breathing going in and out as a relaxing thought. With every exhale, repeat the word "relax."

As common as test anxiety is, it is very possible to overcome it. Make yourself one of the test-takers who overcome this frustrating hindrance.

Additional Bonus Material

Due to our efforts to try to keep this book to a manageable length, we've created a link that will give you access to all of your additional bonus material.

Please visit http://www.mometrix.com/bonus948/osatusohistge to access the information.